as well as the freedom to begin a step-by-step process toward spiritual maturity according to the biblical pattern.

CALLED TO BE FREE will enable you to experience the here-and-now reality of the abundant freedom available to every believer.

About the Author:

BILL COUNTS is director of the Center for Advanced Biblical Studies in Dallas, Texas, sponsored by Probe Ministries International. He previously served as president of Christian Associates Seminary in California and was on the staff of Campus Crusade for Christ. A graduate of Princeton University, he has master's degrees from Southern Methodist University and Dallas Theological Seminary, and has taught at the Rosemead Graduate School of Psychology. Author of THE INCREDIBLE CHRIST and coauthor of FREEDOM FROM GUILT, Counts has also been a contributing editor to *The Journal of Psychology and Theology.*

Called to Be FREE

Called to Be
FREE

BILL COUNTS

FLEMING H. REVELL COMPANY
OLD TAPPAN, NEW JERSEY

Library of Congress Cataloging in Publication Data
Counts, Bill.
    Called to be free.
1. Christian life—1960–   I. Title.
BV4501.2.C684   284.4   80-16534
ISBN 0-8007-0980-2

TO my wife, Beverly

CONTENTS

Foreword

Here is a practical and unique book relating key biblical doctrines to the art of living. In an age characterized by an abundance of human advice and counsel, Bill Counts cuts to the heart of the issue by addressing problems of guilt, forgiveness and self-acceptance in the light of scriptural revelation. He shows, in a very down-to-earth fashion, how a biblical understanding of redemption, conscience, faith, and justification can begin to set us free from the conflicts within our own personalities and between ourselves and others.

This book will be a great aid to new Christians who are looking for an introduction to some of the most important doctrines of the Christian faith. It will also be extremely helpful for those of us who know a lot of doctrine but sometimes have difficulty applying it to our lives. Bill makes doctrine come alive by relating it to the everyday concerns we all face. I highly recommend this, his latest book.

1
THE FIRST STEP TO FREEDOM

ABOUT TWO YEARS AGO, I received a heartbreaking letter:

> Dear Bill:
>
> We are the family your friend David came to live with. Unfortunately, he has taken his own life. Among his possessions we found written instructions to send you this check for two hundred dollars as a contribution to your work. We had hoped he would overcome his depression, but he never did. Death was his goal, but we didn't know it.
>
> We hope to meet you some day. Thank you for your efforts on his behalf.

Outwardly David resembled someone who stepped out of a magazine ad. He was rich, handsome, athletic, and from an Ivy League college. But underneath he was a tortured soul. When he had written me, a few weeks earlier, he was overflowing with hope. Now he was one more suicide statistic.

Then there was Sarah. Her distraught father phoned me, from New Jersey, late one night, and pled with me to see her right away. She was overwhelmed by personal problems, and tomorrow might be too late. Two friends and I raced thirty miles, over the near-empty freeways, to her dingy apartment, where we found an intelligent and attractive, but wretched young woman. We gave what help we could that night, and I met with her several times afterwards. But our efforts were apparently fruitless: She later moved away and, so far as I know, still ekes out a miserable existence.

What causes tragedies like David and Sarah? Why do such people, with every outward advantage, often become wreckage along the roadsides of life? I am convinced that they are people in bondage who need to be set free. The bondage may be inexcusable, irrational, seemingly unexplainable, and strictly of their own making; but they are still in bondage to destructive thought patterns, enslaving habits, and self-defeating life-styles.

Not only do such obvious failures as David and Sarah need to be set free. Those of us less devastated by hang-ups and better able to function also need freedom. We may be somewhat successful; we may be even admired by others, but we know a yawning chasm exists between what we are and what we could be. Though we may not be miserable, we could be much more happy than we are; though our jobs and marriages provide some fulfillment, they could become even more deeply satisfying—not that we will become perfect here and now. But we can experience new degrees of freedom and rise higher than we ever have.

The purpose of this book is to help you experience, more fully than ever, this freedom God wants you to enjoy.

First-Century Redemption

The New Testament repeatediy uses a word which promised freedom to early Christians: *redemption.* We seldom hear this word, except when we redeem stamps received at the supermarket. But in biblical times the word painted a vivid picture in the mind of every hearer.

Millions then were slaves. Sometimes they were forced into slavery because they had committed supposed crimes, as in the movie *Ben Hur,* in which a brick fell from Judah's roof and nearly killed a Roman official. Sometimes people became slaves because their side lost a war, and even distinguished officers might become lowly slaves. Sometimes people sold themselves or family members into slavery, because of debt.

But whereas in the Old South slaves were black, uneducated, and illiterate, slaves in Roman times were of all races, and sometimes they were more talented than their masters. Sometimes they could earn money and buy their freedom. Sometimes their masters set them free. When they were set free, slaves would take money, called the ransom, to a pagan temple and present it to the pagan god. Technically, they were then slaves to the god; actually, they were free men. The Roman Empire brimmed over with ex-slaves, called *freedmen.* One census of Rome revealed that 80 percent of the city was comprised of either slaves or freedmen.

When such people read in the New Testament of ". . . the redemption which is in Christ Jesus" (Romans 3:24), that they were ". . . bought with a price" (1 Corinthians 6:20), and that "If therefore the Son shall make you free, you shall be free indeed" (John 8:36), they were touched to the core of their beings.

But from what did Jesus Christ promise to free these people? Not from the bondage to human masters, but from the even more wretched slavery to destructive drives that ruin people like David and Sarah. The Gospel promised these people freedom from the same anxiety, self-hate, guilt, depression, hostility and purposelessness that plague us today—as well as freedom from an eternity separated from God. At the core of the Christian Good News was a promise of liberation for humankind.

"A Hand Grenade Made Me Do It"

But if Jesus Christ promises abundant freedom, why do we taste so little of it? I believe a major reason is that we attempt to escape responsibility for the sins and faults from which God wants to free us. *The first step toward freedom comes when you accept responsibility for much of your own bondage.*

Recently our local newspaper reported about a man who attempted to rob a jewelry store. The police surrounded the store before he could escape, so he held the employees hostage for five hours, until he finally surrendered. Later he was interviewed and blamed the robbery, plus a string of other crimes and failures, on his Vietnam war experiences. He said a hand-grenade explosion had injured him permanently, caused him to lose emotional stability, and condemned him to a life of crime.

Notice his thinking: *I am not responsible for robbing a jewelry store and holding people hostage; the exploding hand grenade made me do it.* The first people who ever lived shared the same mentality, according to the Book of Genesis. When God asked Adam if he had eaten of the tree of knowledge of good and evil, Adam did not answer, "Yes, I did. I should not have done so. I accept responsibility." Instead he lamely excused himself with ". . . The woman whom thou gavest to be with me, she gave me of the tree, and I did eat" (Genesis 3:12 KJV). Adam was not responsible! Eve made him do it, and since God gave Eve to Adam, really God was the culprit!

On one occasion D. L. Moody, a famous evangelist of the last century, preached in a large city jail. Afterwards, when he went from cell to cell, visiting the prisoners, he found that every man gave a perfect excuse for being in jail. It was his business partner's fault, the government's fault, or the jury's fault. It was always someone else's fault. Finally, Moody came to the last cell, where he found the only man who responded to his sermon. He was also the only one who admitted that being in jail was his own fault!

The Man With a Wooden Leg

Psychiatrist Eric Berne unmasks the same pattern in his book *Games People Play.* He calls various psychological strategies we deceitfully, and often unconsciously, use, "games." One game he names "wooden leg." A man with a wooden leg is a life-long cripple. Berne feels that, emotionally, many people play this game.

A person tells himself, *I am an emotional and spiritual cripple. It's unfair to expect healthy behavior from me. My parents, my circumstances, my genetic makeup: These have ruined my life. What can you expect of a man with a wooden leg?* Because of this, he accepts no responsibility for who he is or for what he can become. He excuses himself from life, as a man with a wooden leg excuses himself from a track meet.

Such evasions of responsibility almost guarantee continued bondage. They carry with them unwritten but devastating messages. One message often is: *Forces outside myself have made me this way. I cannot change unless they change.* More than once, husbands or wives have come to me for counseling, complaining, "I could really be happy and live a good Christian life, if it weren't for my mate." Often the wife says, "My husband is supposed to be the spiritual leader. He never opens a Bible. He doesn't have family devotions. He doesn't like church. Since he gives me no spiritual leadership, how can I be expected to live a Christian life?" A husband laments, in the same way, that his hypocritical wife forever nags and criticizes him. How can he possibly give leadership to such a woman?

The message to the spouse is: "How can you expect anything of me unless *you* change?" If this is true of me, my life is really under the control of other people. I am helpless. *They* have all power over me. My happiness, welfare, and success are all in *their* hands. I have become *their* slaves, and freedom is impossible.

Another message may be: *I have been so hurt by past events and circumstances that I am reduced to helplessness in this area of my life. I can only change if nothing is expected of me, if some outside force or person does it all.* The man with a wooden leg would like to walk normally, but this would only happen if some miracle worker magically gave him a new leg. In the process, nothing would be required of the man, everything of the miracle worker.

But people often say, "Isn't this what Christianity teaches? God does it all; I do nothing?" This is an unfortunate distortion of the truth. Actually God strengthens *me* to do what I need to do. Paul says "*I* can do all things in him who enables *me*" (*see* Philippians 4:13).

Is Some Mental Illness a Myth?

Unfortunately, some psychiatrists and psychologists help keep their patients in such a passive bondage, in my opinion, by terming emotional and spiritual problems that have no known physical causes "illnesses." Certainly emotional problems have some parallels with physical illnesses: Both may cause intense suffering; both may have unknown origins; both may be difficult to cure.

But we usually have little or no responsibility for catching an illness. I may get on an elevator next to someone who has the flu. Before I know it, he has coughed in my direction. A few days later I am flat on my back with a fever, a headache, and a sore throat. How could I know this person had the flu? I did nothing blameworthy to catch the disease; and all I can do, to recover, is lie passively in bed, drink liquids, and take aspirin, until nature takes its course.

When we tell people that their emotional and spiritual problems are illnesses, we convey that they have no responsibility for their problems. They have caught diseases and can do little to get rid of them, except to take some pills and passively submit to the psychiatrist's care, until the ailments go away. Just as a man with the flu would not usually say, "It's my responsibility that I have this flu," but, if anything, would blame the careless person who gave it to him, so the victim of emotional and spiritual illnesses can say, "This problem is not my responsibility. Someone else—probably my father or mother—gave it to me. All I can do is remain its victim, until someday, hopefully, nature takes its course."

Nothing defeats and imprisons people more than this line of thinking! As long as we see ourselves as helpless, nonresponsible, passive victims of what others have done to us, we can never begin to experience the freedom Jesus offers us.

The freedom Jesus offers us is a freedom that comes to people who acknowledge that they have something to do with what they are. They may have had poor home environments; they may have suffered deprived childhoods; they may have received little love; they may not understand the origin of their problems, but still they share a responsibility for what they are.

Certainly the hand grenade was a terrible experience; certainly Eve contributed to Adam's sin; certainly the serpent sowed doubts in Eve's mind, to begin with. But the man has a responsibility for holding up the jewelry store; Adam had a responsibility for eating the fruit; Eve shared the blame for listening to the serpent, and we share responsibility for the choices that have put us where we are.

The Old Testament records how King David seduced Bathsheba, fathered her child, and murdered her husband. God then sent the prophet Nathan to reprimand David. David could have responded, "It is all Bathsheba's fault. She was bathing on the roof of her home, naked. I cannot help myself when I see a beautiful, naked woman. I was forced to seduce her."

The night Peter denied Jesus, he could have protested, "I am an up-and-down person, like a yo-yo. Under the circumstances, having had no sleep, and with my life at stake, it was impossible for me to do anything but bend with the wind. I had to deny Jesus."

"If Only . . ."

The message of this chapter, then, is that the road to free-dom begins with our accepting responsibility before God for who we are and what we can become. We no longer need to come to God with our excuses, saying, "God, I could be a free and happy person if only:

I were married
I could divorce my mate
I had a better job
My father had been a good man
My mother hadn't been an alcoholic
I didn't have to raise a retarded child
I had more money
My health were good

Now it is true such problems make our lives more difficult. God is understanding and compassionate toward those who bear heavy burdens. But freedom still begins when we take responsibility.

Yet, at just this point, our greatest fear comes. If we let go of all our excuses, we might really change and become differ-ent people. Our misery may be painful, but at least it's fa-miliar. But that unknown freedom can be absolutely terrify-ing!

Once Jesus cast thousands of demons out of a man and sent them into a herd of pigs, which ran into the sea (Mark 5:1–20). The frightened citizens united in asking Jesus to leave the area. Though the shrieking, demon-possessed ma-niac, now healed, had terrified them for years, they were used to him. With the demoniac now healed, they ap-parently thought: *What else might happen? Perhaps many other such people will be healed. Perhaps we will have to give up worship of our gods and worship a new God who has such power* [they were apparently pagan gentiles]. *Perhaps this new God will change many of our practices: how we do business, how we treat our families. Perhaps we'll have to become Jews. It's too frightening. We don't want Jesus around.*

For these people, the miserable familiar was preferable to threatening change. So it is for many of us. We are actually afraid to be different. But once we surrender our feeble excuses, reject our rationalizations, and allow the first drops of freedom to flow through our veins, we will find that we need never fear change, when it is for the better.

2
THE FREE FORTUNE

A QUIET CALIFORNIA COMMUNITY overlooking the Pacific recently discovered that perhaps 60 million barrels of oil were trapped underneath its heavy clay soil. Part of the community resembles other middle-class neighborhoods. Post-World War II stucco houses, narrow, tree-lined streets, family-owned businesses, a few gas stations, two grocery stores, and a hardware store give no hint that hundreds of millions of dollars' worth of energy lies buried beneath its parcels of property.

This neighborhood pictures for me one of the great truths of the spiritual life. The Christian appears as an ordinary person just like those middle-class houses. Externally he is no different from others. But a treasure of spiritual resources is available to him, just like the underground oil field. And he needs only to discover and tap these resources that are already there and just waiting to be used.

Paul writes of these resources: "Blessed be the God and Father of our Lord Jesus Christ who has blessed us with *every* spiritual blessing in the heavenly places in Christ Jesus" (*see* Ephesians 1:3). Paul tells his readers that they *already have every spiritual blessing they will ever need in this life.* He says God *has* blessed them, not that He *will* or *may* bless them.

What are spiritual blessings? They are pricelsss benefits that God grants to believers. They are neither material nor visible, but they are as real as our arms and legs and infinitely more important. They include forgiveness (Ephesians 1:7), the presence of the Holy Spirit in our lives (Ephesians 1:13, 14), becoming part of the body of Christ (Ephesians 2), spiritual gifts (Ephesians 4), and many other benefits. Since these blessings are "in Christ," they belong to those who believe in Jesus Christ as Lord and Saviour, not to the world in general.

Universal Blessings

Do all Christians possess these blessings, or do they belong only to the most dedicated? Most biblical scholars feel that Paul's Ephesian letter was circular—sent to churches in Ephesus and several surrounding cities as well. The letter lacks the personal greeting Paul usually inserted when he wrote to only one church, and some ancient manuscripts of the letter have a blank where our Bibles read, ". . . to the saints who are at Ephesus . . ." (Ephesians 1:1). These manuscripts read, "to the saints who are ————." Apparently Paul wrote the letter and scribes made copies, inserting the name of a different city on each reproduction.

This means that the Ephesian letter was directed toward any and every kind of Christian in a broad geographic area, not just a spiritual elite. Paul was telling *all* true believers that they *all* had every blessing they needed. The rest of the New Testament echoes this. Second Peter 1:3 says God "has granted to us *everything* pertaining to life and godliness . . ." *(italics mine)*. Note again God *has* granted everything, not *will* grant everything. That all Christians already possess all they need through Jesus Christ is probably the most important New Testament truth about the spiritual life. Yet because our experiences often seem so contradictory, because we frequently feel so weak and overwhelmed, because we fail

so much and succeed so little, we are often appealed to by er-
roneous teachings on the Christian life—teachings that
promise much and deliver little.

The Spiritual-Elite View

A false teaching known as Gnosticism plagued the early
church. The word *Gnostic* comes from the Greek *gnosis,* which
means "knowledge." The Gnostics boasted of a special
knowledge of God, which they said ordinary Christians
lacked. Gnostics would say to the early Christians, "You may
believe in Jesus Christ and the Bible, but you don't have the
special knowledge God wants you to possess. You should
come to our meetings, study our secret teachings, and then
you'll be enlightened. You will have arrived, as we have."

Paul vehemently opposed this. When Gnostics began to
infiltrate the Colossian church, he wrote to the Christians
there that, in Christ ". . . you have been made complete . . ."
(Colossians 2:10). Though he had probably never visited the
church, he told every Christian there that they were complete simply because they were in Christ. We don't need
Christ *plus* some special teaching or emphasis that a supposedly elite group has. If we are ordinary Christians, we already possess the spiritual resources we need, though we may
not be utilizing them as we should. We have total forgiveness; we have all of the Holy Spirit; we have a future
guaranteed in heaven. But Gnostics insisted that only those
who were in their group were truly in touch with God.

Recently some friends and I were asked to speak with a
minister and two housewives visiting from abroad. The three
told us of spectacular miracles they were performing and announced to us that God had called them to purify the entire
Christian church! As proof of this astounding claim, one of
the women asserted she had the stigmata: the wounds of
Christ miraculously appearing on her hands, feet, and side.

Unfortunately, the minister and the other housewife were deceived. They arrogantly felt they were above all other Christians. They were consumed with visions of grandeur. They had special knowledge, insight, and power, which were theirs alone, like the Gnostics of old.

On another occasion, I encountered a church in Los Angeles that claimed it was the only true church in the city. Their worship, their teaching, and even their name was

The world in general

superior to others. Other Christians would squeeze into
heaven by the skin of their teeth, but this group would
march victoriously in, as God's favorites. Such elitism caters
to human arrogance while ignoring the clear scriptural
teaching that the great gulf that separates men is not between one Christian and another, but between those who
know Christ and those who don't. While some churches and
groups are more healthy and dynamic than others, for any
Christian group to claim that it is *the* true church or *the* instrument of God for purifying all other Christians is the
height of narrowness and conceit. (See how the spiritual elite
view might **be** diagrammed on page 23.)

The Crisis View

Alongside the elitist view of the Christian life is the crisis
view. This view has germs of truth, but many who teach it
try to reduce the whole Christian life to one life-changing
crisis that produces instant maturity and solves all problems.
They fail to see that we progressively lay hold of our spiritual
blessings, over a lifetime, and cannot experience them all at
once. Though we are *given* all we need instantaneously, we
experience it only over time. The oil pump doesn't suck out all
the underground oil in an hour. Oil fields take years to yield
their riches.

The crisis view especially attracts perfectionists who don't
like time and struggle. They want to tie up all loose ends immediately and banish problems and struggles in a day. I recall a perfectionistic young man I talked with who was going
through frequent and painful counseling sessions with a psychiatrist. As he was beginning to face his deep-seated problems, the going got too tough. He quit counseling and began
listening to sermons on the radio, convinced that some
prayer, faith, and a spiritual crisis would quickly solve his
dilemmas.

The crisis takes different forms. Some Christians teach that the crisis must be accompanied by a deeply emotional experience. They say that those who lack this particular experience lack God's full blessing, and we should strive to bring *every* Christian into this type of experience. Others emphasize that insight into a certain truth produces the crisis. The truth may be concerned with the Holy Spirit, or the devil, or identification with Christ, or God's grace, or the church. But the full realization of this truth is *the* answer, they claim, and we should try to instruct *every* Christian in this truth right away. A diagram of the crisis view would be:

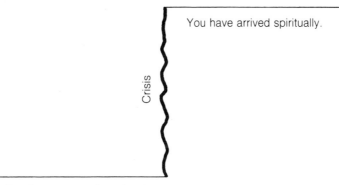

You have arrived spiritually.

Crisis

You live on a mediocre level.

Often books that emphasize a crisis view are heavily autobiographical. The author tells us that he or she was once weak, ineffective, frustrated, and defeated. Then the crisis came, and he or she became a new person.

Is the Crisis View Valid?

I don't entirely discount such experiences. A particular experience or truth may have been the turning point *for them.* But does the Bible guarantee it will be an equal turning point for all Christians, at all times, all over the world? If this were so, we would probably have a very short Bible, with very few pages, presenting only this truth or experience. Anything additional would be unnecessary. Instead the Bible faces us with a rich variety of truths. It discusses the character of God, the person of Jesus Christ, the significance of the cross, the activity of the Holy Spirit, the nature of man, the problem of sin, the relationship of believers to one another, the ethics we should live by, the reality of the devil, the future of our planet, and so on.

Since a variety of people from a variety of backgrounds become believers, is it surprising that a variety of truths and experiences come to us from Scripture, to meet our wide range of needs? For one person the prophecies of the Bible strike a responsive chord, bring him to Christ, and give a sense of urgency to his Christian life. For another, understanding the power of the Holy Spirit is key. For another, who perhaps has delved into the occult, claiming Christ's power over demonic forces is the turning point. For another, sharing experiences in small groups are the watershed. We need to understand all the basic truths of Christianity, but usually certain truths will speak to our needs at certain times, and this is what God intends.

Jesus once healed a blind man by putting mud on his eyes and making him walk half a mile to wash it off in the pool of Siloam (John 9). But in another instance Jesus healed a blind man named Bartimaeus, simply by telling him that he was healed (Mark 10:46–52). Now suppose the blind man healed in the pool of Siloam decided that all blind people should be healed in such a fashion. Why not? This was how he was healed. He would establish the Siloamite denomination for the blind and order his followers to put mud on their eyes and wash it off in the pool of Siloam. Then suppose Bartimaeus decided to set up another denomination for the blind, called the Bartimaeans. Members would receive healing by waiting on God, and no outward action.

No doubt the Siloamites would say to the Bartimaeans, "You are lazy: you just want to sit and have God do everything. You are also proud; it's humbling to cover your eyes with mud." The Bartimaeans would reply, "You are superstitious. You must have this secret mud and go to a pool. But we believe Almighty God doesn't need such things. We believe healing comes by faith and faith alone."

The two would compete with and attack each other. Why? Because they each demand that God work according to a stereotyped crisis experienced by the founder. Unfortunately, just such thinking lies behind many divisions and rivalries in Christendom today.

Variety Is the Spice of Life

In my own life, different truths at different times have unlocked special doors. My first year as a Christian was miserable, until, at a conference, I heard about surrendering every area of life to Jesus Christ. This truth dramatically changed me. A few years later, I was trying as hard as I knew to serve God, but was defeated, frustrated, and fruitless, when I learned to trust the Holy Spirit more and experienced new release from years of frustration. Several years later I felt guilty and depressed for many months, though I outwardly appeared to be a good Christian. Then I got deeper insight into God's grace, and an unbearable burden was lifted. On another occasion I came into contact with small sharing groups. I had always kept my struggles to myself. I never shared them, not even with my wife. Through this small-group experience I learned to share my struggles with others, and a new dimension of living opened for me. I am thankful for all these experiences. Each was what I needed at that time, and each produced enduring results. But no one of these truths solved it all for me, nor will any single solution work for anyone else.

The Bible contains a variety of solutions for a variety of human needs. No one truth can bear the weight of solving everything. Protein is essential in our diets, but a protein-only diet would eventually kill you. You need a balanced diet, both physically and spiritually.

The Progressive View

I believe that the correct view of the Christian life is progressive. Through time, teaching, and experience, we mature and progressively utilize our resources in Christ, though we encounter important crises and turning points along the way. No one reaches physical maturity in a day. The three-month-old baby in the crib does not become a two-hundred-eighty-pound professional football player in a week. Growth takes time.

In college, I recall studying the famous Louisiana Purchase. This transaction took place in 1803, when America bought, from France, much of the midwestern and western United States. What a treasure house of land, forests, mountains, lakes, rivers, and mineral resources became ours, with the stroke of a pen! But though our government gained the land in a moment of time, years were consumed exploring, discovering, and utilizing all that was there, and the task is still not complete. Though the land was ours, we could only possess and utilize it piece by piece, over many years.

In the Old Testament, when Israel entered the land of Canaan, God did not give it to them instantly. They had to conquer it parcel by parcel. They crossed the River Jordan, they took Jericho, then they took a city called Ai, then they defeated the Canaanite armies at Gibeon. God promised the whole land to Israel in a moment of time, but He only gave it to them over the years. As they conquered different portions, they confronted crises, lessons, and experiences of enduring value. So it is with us. We progressively grow; in time, we open ourselves up to what God has given us in eternity. This was Paul's experience, too. He told the Philippians, after he had been a Christian almost thirty years: "Not that I have already . . . become perfect, but I press on in order that I may lay hold of that for which I was laid hold of by Christ Jesus" (Philippians 3:12). He pictures himself as a runner in a race, heading for the finish line and the prize, but he's not there yet. He wrote the Romans, when he had been a Christian twenty-five years, that ". . . we ourselves, having the first fruits of the Spirit, even we ourselves groan within ourselves, waiting eagerly for our adoption as sons, the redemption of our body" (Romans 8:23). Paul longed for the perfection of the resurrection. He was not there yet, and so experienced "groaning" and "weakness" (Romans 8:26). Paul also

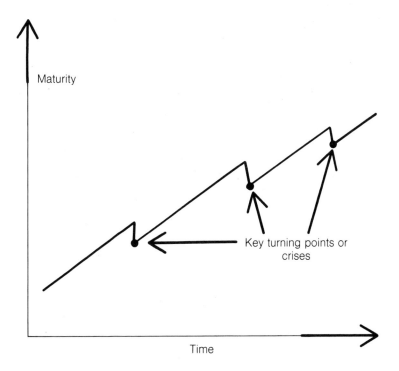

Maturity

Key turning points or crises

Time

warned Timothy about those who taught the dangerous heresy that ". . . the resurrection has already taken place . . ." (2 Timothy 2:18). These false teachers evidently claimed that they were already resurrected, perfect people!

Even though Jesus was sinless from birth, Luke tells us that He ". . . grew in wisdom . . ." (Luke 2:52 NIV), and the author of Hebrews says that He prayed ". . . with loud crying and tears . . ." and ". . . learned obedience from the things which He suffered . . ." (Hebrews 5:7, 8). The idea of a struggle-free, pain-free, instantaneous entrance into spiritual completeness was not even Jesus' experience. Much less will it be ours. (See diagram of the progressive view on page 29.)

Though such a road to growth is neither as quick nor as easy as we might like, I am convinced it is the biblical way and the way that pays off in the end. On several occasions I have encountered older Christians who have grown steadily through the years and learned, step-by-step, the lessons God had for them. Such lives have a special quality about them: a mature wisdom, a genuine piety, a deep faith, an unflagging devotion that money cannot buy. Why settle for less?

3
FINAL FORGIVENESS

OVER A HUNDRED YEARS AGO, the finest and most reputable women of Cincinnati boycotted a local park. The reason? A sign in the park portrayed a Swiss peasant girl with her ankles exposed! Our Victorian forefathers were so straitlaced that they refused to use words like *corset* and *leg* in mixed company. Some of them even spoke of the four *limbs* on a piano; and, at one girls' school, the piano "limbs" were covered with cloth, to make sure no visiting young man was reminded of a girl's legs by gazing at the legs of the baby grand!

Such a prudish society would understandably create guilt-ridden people. In our permissive society, where sleeping together is a standard practice from high school on and where slick pornography is available at every newsstand, guilt should have vanished long ago. But it hasn't. Feelings of guilt, self-hatred, and inadequacy probably plague us more than they did our overmodest grandparents.

I vividly recall counseling a young woman who pulled back her sleeve and displayed gashes she had carved on her arm, with a razor, the night before. Her intense guilt and self-hate unleashed themselves by causing her to slice her own flesh. The detailed causes of the guilt which ravages so many human lives is worth a book in itself (*see* Bruce Narramore and Bill Counts, *Freedom From Guilt* [Irvine, CA: Harvest

House, 1976]). But, in general, guilt is a consequence of our fallenness. We have enough of God's image left in us to sense we are not what we should be. We intuitively know that hostility, selfishness, deceit, arrogance, and hypocrisy—in ourselves and others—are wrong. When such behavior creates pain and frustration, we realize, even more, how far short we fall.

Can Christianity Increase Guilt?

When we believe in Jesus Christ, ideally our guilt feelings should disappear. But, as we discard our former hazy moral standards for the clear and sure precepts of the Bible, our sense of guilt often increases. We have more to fail over than ever before.

Before I found Christ, I obviously never tried to tell someone else to become a Christian. But, a few months after my conversion, guilt feelings began to well up within me. Why wasn't I telling more of my friends? Why hadn't I written my brother about Christ? Like most people, I often felt inadequate and insecure before I believed in Christ. But after trusting Him and learning all that was now expected of me, I felt more guilty and inadequate than ever!

In seeking relief from guilt, multitudes turn to psychiatrists or psychologists. Yet often they find that the professional they seek help from is riddled with guilt himself. As a student of mental health, the professional should expect some mental health in himself. But he often finds that the neurotic and destructive patterns that destroy his patients debilitate him, too, though he should know better. Frequently, he discovers he can help neither his patients nor himself, so his guilt grows along with theirs.

In biblical times people did not consult psychiatrists, of course, so they sought other ways to cast off their burdens of guilt. Gentiles in those days expressed some of their guilt through fear of what their deities would do to them. They believed their gods and goddesses were angry, moody, and manipulative, so the people constantly sought to pacify them. Every disaster was a sign the gods were angry. When an earthquake, flood, or plague struck, or if a child died, or a father injured himself in the fields, it was because the gods were upset. To placate them, people practiced numerous superstitious acts, engaged in bizarre religious rites, and offered countless animal sacrifices. The Greeks called such an animal sacrifice, offered at a pagan temple, the *hilasterion.*

The Jewish Answer

Ancient Jews dismissed such superstitions. The God of the Old Testament was righteous, holy, and constant. Nevertheless, Israel had more than once tasted His anger, as when He sent her, captive, into Babylon. To help ward off the wrath of a righteous God, Israel kept a sacred festival, called *Yom Kippur,* the Day of Atonement. On this day the Jewish high priest would choose two goats, lay his hands on one of them (called the scapegoat), confess the sins of the people, and send it into the wilderness. The goat symbolically bore the sins of the people away and thus acted out their forgiveness.

Before sending the scapegoat away, the high priest took the other goat into the most sacred part of the Jewish temple, called the Holy of Holies, which he could enter only on this day, once a year. The priest would sacrifice the goat and sprinkle its blood on top of a small piece of furniture shaped like a rectangular box, called the ark. The lid of the ark, where the blood was sprinkled, was decorated with two carved, hovering, angelic figures. This lid was called the mercy seat, because here God met the high priest, accepted the blood of the animal sacrifice, and bestowed forgiveness on Israel. In the Greek translation of the Old Testament, the word for "mercy seat" is also *hilasterion.*

The Final Answer

In Romans 3:24, 25 Paul writes of ". . . Christ Jesus whom God displayed publicly as a propitiation in His blood through faith. . . ." The word *propitiation* is again the word *hilasterion.* When a first-century gentile believer read that word, he thought of those worthless sacrifices offered in pagan temples to appease angry gods. Then he thought of Jesus Christ, whose genuine sacrifice forever appeased the anger of a righteous God over sin. In place of useless super-stitions, a real Saviour had offered Himself to a real God, to bring a real forgiveness.

When a first-century Jewish believer read Paul's words, he thought of the yearly Yom Kippur offering. Such offerings never ultimately satisfied God, for the writer of Hebrews tells us, ". . . it is impossible for the blood of bulls and goats to take away sins" (Hebrews 10:4). Animal blood could never solve such a fundamental problem of human existence! But as the Jew read about Jesus Christ as the *hilasterion,* he would realize that a forgiveness that the mercy seat of the ark illus-trated and prophesied, but never accomplished, was now here. Jesus' sacrifice was the basis of forgiveness, and, be-cause it really paid the debt, it needed no repetition, like the yearly Yom Kippur offerings. Hebrews 9:25, 26 claims it is unnecessary that Jesus ". . . should offer Himself often. . . . Otherwise, He would have needed to suffer often since the foundation of the world; but now once at the consummation He has been manifested to put away sin by the sacrifice of Himself." Hebrews 10:18 adds, "Now where there is forgive-ness of these things, there is no longer any offering for sin." Just as you would not make monthly payments on a car you owned free and clear, the Jews needed to offer no more sacrifices to cleanse sins God had already wiped away.

Righteousness and Pity

Jesus' *hilasterion* makes our forgiveness eternal and secure. Sometimes we imagine that God forgives us only out of pity. Because He is loving and merciful, He sent Christ to die for us. But once Christ suffered for us, our forgiveness rests not even on God's pity, but on the objective, historical sacrifice of Christ. This is why 1 John 1:9 says "If we confess our sins, He is faithful and righteous to forgive us our sins and to cleanse us from all unrighteousness." John says that God forgives us, not from pity, but from faithfulness and righteousness. If He didn't forgive us, He would renege on His promise to take our sins away through Christ, and He would become unfaithful. He would also reject the righteous sacrifice of His own Son, offered in our place. The very character of God demands that we be forgiven.

Perhaps no Old Testament event illustrates our forgiveness as well as the Jews' escape from Egypt, under Moses. Before Israel escaped the clutches of the evil Pharaoh, each Jew had to put blood on his doorposts, so the death angel would pass over his house without killing his firstborn son. This was the first Passover, which the Jews commemorated with a feast. God promised, ". . . when I see the blood I will pass over you . . ." (Exodus 12:13).

Suppose, at the Exodus, God had changed His mind and had decided, "I will kill the Israelite children, too, regardless of the blood and My promise." Then God would have become a liar and denied the adequacy of the sacrifice He Himself ordered.

But when the angel of death saw the lamb's blood on the door, he passed over and did not kill. Perhaps an Israelite could have said, "I love God deeply; I feel very close to Him, but it's too uncouth to put blood on my doorpost! I just won't do it." He would have lost his eldest son. Perhaps another Israelite could have said, "I don't feel much love for God; I feel very distant from Him, but I'll still put the blood on the doorpost." His son would have been spared, for it was not feelings, piety, or good deeds that saved the Israelite; it was only the blood. In the same way, Jesus' death for us, received through faith, brings forgiveness—not our feelings, piety, or works—only His blood.

God Is Satisfied, but We Aren't

Even though Jesus died for our sins, in our fallenness, we tend to devalue what He has done. God is satisfied with Jesus' death for us, but often we are not. As a result, subtle and devastating behavior patterns erupt, which become attempts to pay ourselves back, when Jesus has already paid it all.

A pattern popular in Christendom and most religions down through the ages is asceticism. Asceticism is the denial of legitimate physical needs for supposedly spiritual purposes. One of the most famous ascetics was Saint Simeon Stylites, who lived in the fifth century. Saint Simeon distinguished himself by building a platform about three feet in circumference and eventually sixty feet off the ground, where he lived for twenty-nine years. He rarely came down or bathed and was covered with vermin and sores. Today we would probably institutionalize him. Instead the church canonized him. For years Saint Simeon's wretched followers, known as pillar saints, copied their master by living out hideous existences. In coldest winter or hottest summer, in rain or drought, these sincere but deceived "saints" were always visible atop their pillars.

What drove Saint Simeon and the pillar saints to such extremes? Certainly guilt was an element. Saint Simeon punished himself, instead of understanding that God had punished Christ for him.

Another pattern is accident proneness. I once counseled an older woman and noticed she seemed physically uncomfortable. She told me her leg hurt. When I asked why her leg hurt, she told me it resulted from a car wreck. When I asked about the car wreck, she told me it occurred when she was on the way to the hospital. When I asked why she went to the hospital, she said it was because she had fallen off her porch. As we talked more, it became apparent that her life was a long string of disasters. Some of these may have been by chance, but many seemed unconsciously self-caused. Secretly she seemed to want to punish herself, so she had one accident after another.

"They're Out to Get Me!"

Others follow a paranoid pattern. Their guilt feelings are so intense they cannot accept them, so they project them onto others. In their inner selves they feel dirty, terrible, and inadequate. But instead of admitting to these feelings, they imagine that everyone else feels that way about them. They feel everyone is suspicious of them and against them.

I recall a particularly sad case of an attractive and intelligent middle-aged woman who began hearing voices. She was convinced an electronic speaker system secretly planted in her home by her scientist husband was producing the voices, which would say, "You're filthy, you're terrible, you're sexually impure," and would call her dirty names. She sought out the police to get relief from her husband's supposed harassment. In reality, of course, her own feelings of guilt, failure, and inadequacy were harassing her. The voices were not from speakers; they were from deep within her own soul.

"I'm Worthless"

Perhaps the most common expression of guilt is depression. We all know the inner voice that says, "You're worthless; you're no good; you're a real loser." Several years ago a close friend was walking past a Santa Monica hotel when he noticed a crowd on the sidewalk. He looked up and saw a girl ready to jump. Quickly he raced into the hotel and jumped in the elevator. He got out on her floor, saw her at the end of the hall, and edged toward her. In a soft voice he said, "Miss, God loves you." Her face contorted, and she jumped to her death on the hard concrete below.

Engulfed in self-hate and overwhelmed by depression, she destroyed herself rather than accept that God had, in a sense, "destroyed" Jesus in her place. Depression is often self-punishment. We psychologically beat ourselves to pulps, and sometimes, as in the case of this girl, physically destroy ourselves, as well.

Such depression is not the Holy Spirit's convicting work! The Holy Spirit's goal is our improvement, not our destruction. He convicts one of a *specific* sin of which he can repent. Paul rejoiced that the Corinthians ". . . were made sorrowful to the point of repentance . . ." (2 Corinthians 7:9). When David seduced Bathsheba and murdered Uriah, her husband, Nathan the prophet confronted David specifically: ". . . You have struck down Uriah the Hittite with the sword, have taken his wife to be your wife, and have killed him. . ." (2 Samuel 12:9). David could and did repent of this specific action.

The goal of guilt-induced depression is our punishment, not our improvement. This feeling that one is a no-good loser is so broad and vague that no repentance is possible. One would have to become a different person to solve the problem. Since this is impossible, the depressed man wallows in self-pity and usually behaves even worse, since his situation seems hopeless. In an extreme case he may even decide to end it all. We might diagram it this way:

Conviction

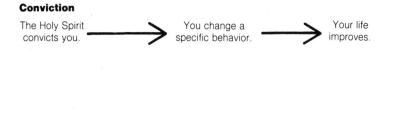

The Holy Spirit convicts you. → You change a specific behavior. → Your life improves.

Depression

Guilt feelings punish you. → You feel rejected. → Your life gets worse—possible self-destruction.

Depression and these other strategies are just some of the ways we try to pay ourselves back, instead of accepting that God paid Jesus in our place. One of the most important milestones on the road to freedom is accepting our own forgiveness. We must believe that God has made it total, final, and irreversible. Jesus has paid it *all*.

When we believe on Jesus Christ, we find a solution for guilt that no one outside of Christ can offer. We do not become perfect, but, at long last, we become forgiven.

4
YOU DON'T ALWAYS GET WHAT YOU EARN

A RECENT NEWSPAPER PHOTO showed two twelve-year-old girls side by side—one gleeful and happy, the other sobbing, her face buried in her hands. The smiling girl had just won a national spelling contest. The sobbing one had just lost. As my wife and I discussed the picture, she remarked, "Life's like that. Some win and some lose." Indeed it is. Our competitive society produces many winners, but often there are more losers. In first grade, agile and coordinated little Johnny is always chosen first for any sports team, while fat and slow Howard is chosen last. But when the class is tested for intelligence, Howard may be put in a gifted program, while Johnny ends up with the slow learners. In high school the beautiful and poised Sally is everyone's favorite, while homely Joan's acne-marred complexion keeps her from ever having a date. Sam, brilliant and capable in college, enters medical school, graduates at the top of his class, and becomes a wealthy neurosurgeon. His college buddy, Fred, goes from job to job, becomes a heavy drinker, and winds up on skid row.

You often get out of life what you put into it. Brains, work, looks, and a little luck put you at the top. The opposite puts you at the bottom.

A Different Kingdom

But Jesus told Pontius Pilate, ". . . My kingdom is not of this world . . ." (John 18:36). He said His ways were not the world's ways, and nowhere is the contrast more stark than in the biblical teaching on God's grace.

The Greek word for grace is *charis,* which means "favor." When an ancient ruler bestowed benefits on his subjects, he was bestowing *charis.* These egotistic rulers often arbitrarily bestowed favor or punishment. A king or emperor might order a subject executed on only a whim. When Herod the Great heard about Jesus' birth, he ordered the slaughter of all infants in Bethlehem two years old and under—without the modern politician's concern about courts, laws, the press, or the citizens. He just did it. But, just as arbitrarily, a ruler might bestow generous favors on his subjects: Roman citizenship, tax relief, new buildings, government jobs. All such favors were *charis.* The favors might or might not be earned; their bestowal depended more on the wish of the ruler than the merit of his subjects.

No Obligations

When Paul described God's grace, he chose the word *charis,* perhaps because it suggested that bestowal of favor depended on the giver and not the recipient. In Romans 9:15 he quotes what God said to Moses: ". . . I will have mercy on whom I have mercy, and I will have compassion on whom I have compassion." God owes us no debts. The source of His favors lies in Him, not in us.

Paul insists on this. When he speaks of the Jewish remnant God is rescuing in this age, he says, ". . . if it is by grace, it is no longer on the basis of works [that is, earned by their efforts], otherwise grace is no longer grace" (Romans 11:6). *Charis* cannot be earned; what is earned cannot be *charis.*

Jesus once told a parable of farm hands who contracted with a vineyard owner for the equivalent of twenty dollars for one day's work (Matthew 20:1–16). Late in the day, the owner recruited additional laborers, who worked only one or two hours, instead of all day, like the others. At day's end he gave those who worked a few hours the same amount he gave to those who worked all day. Those who worked all day naturally complained.

But the owner replied, ". . . I wish to give to this last man the same as to you. Is it not lawful for me to do what I wish with what is my own? Or is your eye envious [that is, are you envious] because I am generous?" (Matthew 20:14, 15). The owner had kept his bargain with those who worked all day, but, because he was generous, bestowed undeserved money on those who worked one hour. This was *charis*.

A Mechanic Who Worked Late

Years ago I was driving across the barren California desert, late one Sunday afternoon, heading to Texas, for my wedding. Suddenly, my motor began pinging noisily. I drove into a service station and found that some oil lines in the engine were clogged. It was near closing time, and the mechanic could have told me to find a motel and return the next day. But, when he realized my urgent need to arrive in Texas on time, he stayed open several extra hours, missed his dinner, and fixed my car for the regular rate. This was *charis*—an undeserved kindness.

God has always been a God of *charis*. In the Old Testament, God revealed Himself to Abraham and promised him a land, a multitude of descendants, and worldwide blessing through these descendants. Did Abraham deserve this? Not at all—God could have let this man live out an obscure life and die childless, one more unremembered citizen of a forgotten civilization.

But God dealt with Abraham in *charis*. Later God took Abraham's offspring, the people of Israel, rescued them from Egypt, and gave them the Old Testament Law. This was also an act of *charis.* The Old Testament Law was never intended to save these people for heaven. If followed, it certainly would have given them a better life on earth, for its rules reflected divine wisdom for the social, spiritual, and moral life of a nation. But it could not offer permanent forgiveness and, in Paul's words, was only a "tutor" to eventually bring the nation to Christ (Galatians 3:24).

By the times of Jesus, the Jewish rabbis had so distorted the Old Testament Law that they refused to see God as the bestower of *charis* on the undeserving and the Law as Israel's temporary guide until the Gospel came. They insisted that God owed the Jewish people the first stage of salvation for simply being Jewish, the second stage for obeying the Law and countless additional rules of the Pharisees, and the final stage for repenting of all mistakes. From start to finish, the Jew earned his salvation.

Jesus, Paul, and the New Testament writers took issue with this view. They taught that God saved through *charis,* not law keeping: "For by grace [*charis*] you have been saved through faith;" Paul wrote, ". . . it is the gift of God, not as a result of works, that no one should boast" (Ephesians 2:8, 9).

He Was Once Like an Army Sergeant

In 1967 I attended a large gathering of the staff members of the Christian organization I was then working for. I felt depressed and guilty, though my life was free from what would be called blatant sin. In fact, I was praying, reading my Bible, and engaged in evangelistic work. But when I compared the results of my ministry with the results of others and the results I felt I should be getting, I felt like a failure. One night I prayed and asked God to show me why I felt so depressed.

The next morning one of our staff directors spoke. This

man had previously reminded me of an army sergeant giving orders, for he seemed to have no understanding of weakness or failure, and his usual solution to problems was to try harder. But on that morning, his talk was different from anything I had ever heard him say. He spoke of God's love and acceptance, of working from God's grace, not for it.

I felt he was speaking to no one but me. I realized that, though I was relying on Jesus Christ and grace to make me acceptable for heaven, I was relying on myself and successful ministry endeavors to become acceptable on earth. I felt God didn't fully accept me in this life, because I lacked the faith, courage, and dedication of others. In reality, of course, many of my fellow workers felt the same toward me: They imagined my faith and dedication were superior to theirs, so they considered themselves failures, compared to me. I saw that, in spite of my faults and failures, God accepted me right then, because of grace: *charis.* I saw that the Bible teaches we work *from* our acceptance, but never *for* it.

Jesus and Grace

Jesus' ministry constantly illustrates *charis.* When the Pharisees dragged an immoral woman before Him and demanded her execution, as prescribed by Moses' law, He rebuffed them (John 8:1–11). Her unworthy accusers actually cared little about stamping out immorality. Their real motive was to discredit Jesus' love for sinners by making Him appear as one who refused to enforce Moses' commands. His stern rebuke, ". . . He who is without sin among you, let him be the first to throw a stone at her" (John 8:7), sent the Pharisees off in disarray. Jesus then told the woman He did not condemn her and said ". . . go your way; from now on sin no more" (John 8:11). This immoral woman deserved condemnation. Instead Jesus gave her *charis,* undeserved favor.

But, because of this grace, she was to clean up her life, so Jesus said she should no longer live in immorality. The woman was to work *from* acceptance, not *for* it.

On another occasion Jesus invited Himself into the home of Zaccheus, the tax collector. Ancient tax collectors originally were paid by commission, so, the more money they gouged out of citizens, the wealthier they became. Since they were usually deceitful and dishonest, their fellow Jews despised them and prohibited them from attending the synagogue. Yet Jesus loved Zaccheus and risked His reputation to spend the night with Zaccheus' family. As a result Zaccheus repented of his crooked ways and announced, ". . . half of my possessions I will give to the poor, and if I have defrauded anyone of anything, I will give back four times as much" (Luke 19:8). Zaccheus deserved condemnation. Instead he got grace. But his life changed, because he could work *from* acceptance, not *for* it.

Paul followed Jesus' example. He wrote the Romans, "I urge you therefore, brethren, by the mercies of God, to present your bodies a living and holy sacrifice . . ." (Romans 12:1). For eleven chapters he had unfolded to the Romans the wonders of God's grace and salvation. On this basis he exhorted them to live the Christian life. But they were to work from this grace and salvation, not for it. He says, "I urge you *therefore* [that is, because of all God has done] . . ." (*italics mine*).

The World in Reverse

Our grace relationship with God is the reverse of most human relationships. We earn job promotions through good work. We attract close friends through our personalities, interests, and achievements. We even gain mates through proving physically and emotionally pleasing to the opposite sex. I don't know that we can always operate differently on the human level, but we certainly should with God.

Perhaps the one human relationship that most nearly reflects grace is the one between parents and small children. Cute though they are, small children do little to earn their parents' love. Little children awaken them early, never thinking, *Daddy and Mommy work so hard; they must be exhausted. I'll let them get a couple of hours of well-earned rest.* At bedtime, they never say, "Mommy, you've had a hard day. I'll go to bed early so you can have some time for yourself." Even though they are usually thoughtless, inconsiderate, and selfish—behavior we hate to tolerate in adults—we love our children and make almost any sacrifice for them. This does not mean we don't care whether they're good or bad, of course. We do. But we love them, regardless. This pictures in miniature God's grace toward us all.

Mistaken Motives

As we begin to fathom God's grace, we also begin to live the Christian life from the highest motives: love and thankfulness. Unfortunately, many attempt to obey God for lesser reasons and lose out in the long run. Fear of negative consequences motivates some. They fear that disobedience will keep them out of heaven or that sin will bring disastrous results into their lives. We actually do reap what we sow, and sin does bring disastrous results, as the next chapter shows. But this is an inferior motive for Christian living and often breaks down when we feel we might escape some of the negative consequences we really deserve.

Sam has an unhappy marriage. He flirts with his cute and vivacious secretary, but fears further involvement, because, if his vindictive wife finds out, she will divorce him, slander him, and financially ruin him. But when he encounters sexual temptation on a business trip abroad, he quickly gives in, since chances are his wife and friends will never discover his immoral behavior. Sam's behavior is really amoral, based only on immediate consequences, not eternal principles of right and wrong. He is like the criminal held in check only when he knows swift and sure punishment will strike.

An employee of a Christian organization embezzled several thousand dollars. The scheme was so clever that he was only caught when his misappropriations were accidentally uncovered. This employee regretted only that he was found out, not that he had stolen money. Fear of negative consequences, not love of God, motivated him. When, through a clever trick, it appeared he could escape punishment, dishonesty became acceptable behavior. Sometime you might ask yourself, *If I knew for sure I could get away with some sin—no one would know and I would not suffer—would I still refrain from it?*

Another inferior motive is the desire to please others. Jesus condemned the Pharisees because they "practiced their righteousness before men to be noticed by them" (*see* Matthew 6:1). Paul warned Christian slaves against obeying their masters with ". . . external service, as those who merely please men . . ." (Colossians 3:22). I once knew of a college student who boasted to other Christian students that he had converted scores of others to the Christian faith. Every week he would tell how he had successfully evangelized someone. It turned out that he never told anyone about his faith. He manufactured the stories to gain admiration. We naturally want to please others; but, when we make this our major motivation, our lives become hypocritical facades. When others' admiration vanishes, our basis for following God collapses. No doubt droves of professing believers today would leave the church tomorrow if Christianity suddenly became unpopular in America.

The Guilt Trap

Often we try to motivate ourselves or others through guilt. Since our sins are atoned for by Christ and not by our works, this is unnecessary and often disastrous. A Texas housewife complained to me that her husband gave no spiritual leadership to the family, though he was chairman of the church board. She tried to correct his faults through administering frequent doses of guilt and regularly chided him for not conducting family devotions, not studying the Bible, not disciplining the children properly, not spending his money wisely, and so on. Several months after our conversation, both she and the church were shocked when he ran off with another woman. Her continual use of guilt backfired by triggering open rebellion.

An exasperated Florida pastor sought my advice because his deacons and elders were uncooperative. They required his incessant exhortation to accomplish even menial tasks such as getting the church lawn mowed. Somehow the relationship had evolved into his playing the role of a nagging parent, while the church boards acted the part of irresponsible children who needed scolding. These deacons and elders unconsciously rebelled at the pastor's motivating them through guilt. They would verbally agree to fulfill responsibilities, but resisted carrying out the assigned tasks.

Guilt usually provokes the opposite of the behavior we desire. We should not live with guilt ourselves, nor should we use it on others. We should correct and exhort each other without berating, humiliating, nagging, or creating the roles of scolding parents for ourselves and irresponsible children for others.

Ultimately I should live for God because I love Him; am thankful to Him; and, of my own choice, desire to follow His will. Whether following God brings pleasure or pain is not the point. Whether others admire or despise me is irrelevant. Love for God motivated the early Christians, and their faith survived persecution and peril. All the hostile forces in the world cannot stamp out a Christianity motivated by God's indescribable grace.

5

THE LAW OF LOGICAL CONSEQUENCES

A LADERA HEIGHTS, California, woman was recently convicted of welfare fraud amounting to nearly $290,000. She was charged with opening welfare accounts under ten different names and listing thirty fictitious children for whom she received money. When arrested, she lived in a $170,000 home and owned a new Cadillac and late-model Mustang, while her daughter drove a new Porsche. Up to that time, she had perpetrated the largest known welfare swindle in American history.

Though the welfare system is supposed to aid the destitute, this woman abused it to live like a queen, using funds intended for the poor to her personal advantage. Unfortunately, our permissive society pressures us to respond to the Christian life in the same way. Instead of using grace to salvage ourselves from the ghetto of destructive living, we may misuse it for our own self-indulgence; instead of allowing grace to bring freedom *from* sin, we may twist it into the freedom *to* sin.

The Scriptures denounce such heresy. Jude condemns those who ". . . turn the grace of our God into licentiousness . . ." (Jude 4), and Paul lashes out at those who teach we may ". . . continue in sin that grace might increase" (Romans 6:1). Yet only authentic grace teaching yields to such perversion. Only the genuine Gospel with a slight, but fatal, shift degenerates into full-blown license. Some time ago a young Missouri housewife wrote:

> Dear Bill Counts,
>
> I have read one of your books, and you don't know all the trouble it has gotten me into! I attend a local church where they do nothing but emphasize guilt and condemnation. They tell me that total forgiveness just through faith in Jesus Christ is some kind of heresy.
>
> Recently they told me that, unless I live up to all the rules of this church, I will not go to heaven. They have even said if I leave their church I will probably go to hell. I told them your book said the opposite, but they think it's heresy, too.
>
> I am frustrated, confused, and don't know what to do. Am I really forgiven for all my sins just by trusting in Jesus Christ? Should I stay in this church? Please write and give me some help.

Too Little Grace

If this woman's letter accurately reflects her church's teachings, not enough grace dribbles into that congregation to turn into licentiousness! Such a rule-laden, fear-filled, judgment-centered Christianity can never be misconstrued, as Paul's message was, as freedom to live in sin. Only the New Testament message that God offers unearned forgiveness to sinful people can be perverted into license for unrestrained rebellion. This doesn't mean that genuine grace promotes sin, of course, while a message of condemnation produces righteousness. Just the opposite is true. The condemnation approach apparently used by this church eventually makes people worse, according to Paul, for such an ingredient in Moses' Law made "transgression increase" and caused Israel to rebel to the limit (Romans 5:20). We must live with the tension that God forgives all our sins, but still expects us not to sin, if we are to live with New Testament Christianity.

But since New Testament Christianity is so easily misinterpreted, we must delve more deeply into why Christians under grace should not sin. A major reason is that, though grace delivers from sin's eternal condemnation, it does not deliver from sin's logical consequences. If you place your hand on a hot stove, you get burned. If you refuse to brush your teeth, you get cavities. If you walk off a building, you plummet to the sidewalk. These natural consequences occur, whether we are criminals or saints, because physical laws function without respect of persons. We also operate under divinely established moral laws that likewise function without respect of persons.

Though God sometimes delays or decreases sin's ruinous results, He never deletes them. We are *never* better off living rebelliously rather than righteously.

Reaping the Bitter Harvest

Everywhere Scripture testifies that whoever plants the seeds of iniquity will one day harvest its bitter fruit. The Psalmist writes that the sinful man "... has dug a pit and hollowed it out, And has fallen into the hole which he made. His mischief will return upon his own head ..." (Psalms 7:15, 16). The Book of Job warns that "... those who plow iniquity And those who sow trouble harvest it" (Job 4:8). Proverbs cautions that the rebellious "... shall eat of the fruit of their own way ..." (Proverbs 1:31).

The New Testament echoes the same theme. In Romans 1:18 Paul says "For the wrath of God is revealed from heaven against all ungodliness and unrighteousness of men. . . ." Biblical scholars have noted that Paul wrote God's wrath *is* revealed, not *will be* revealed. His wrath falls on the rebellious right now. How? The rest of this chapter in Romans provides the key. It spells out how God handed over the sinful and God-rejecting people of that day to the natural consequences of their actions. Their denial of God led to polytheistic idolatry, superstition, sexual perversion, cruelty, family collapse, and every kind of evil, until the Roman Empire became like a savage jungle.

God has so constructed the universe that His wrath against sin shows itself through the natural results that follow sin. Rebellion against God sooner or later brings automatic suffering and misery. Though, in the future, God will also show His wrath against sin in a final judgment, He presently shows His wrath against sin in the disastrous difficulties the rebellious person brings on himself and those around him. Though spared God's eternal and personal wrath, a believer who enters into the world's sinful ways tastes the bitter dregs of this present, impersonal wrath built into the fabric of human existence.

The same thought underlies Paul's statement to the Galatians, "Do not be deceived, God is not mocked; for whatever a man sows, this he will also reap. For the one who sows to his own flesh shall from the flesh reap corruption . . ." (Galatians 6:7, 8). Though the context of this passage is giving money, the law of sowing and reaping extends to all of life: ". . . *whatever* a man sows, this he will also reap" *(italics mine)*.

Everywhere the Scripture associates unhappiness, misery, misfortune, destruction, and finally death with sin. *Nowhere* is it linked with true and lasting happiness. At best, sin's quickly fading pleasures soon turn into compounded, long-term pain.

Since, at its core, sin is painful, destructive, and damaging, can we justify indulging in it, because, "God forgives us, anyhow"? We cannot drink poison and not hurt our stomachs; we cannot walk through fire and stay unburned; we cannot stare at the sun and keep our eyesight. We cannot live in sin and remain happy and satisfied. Though God may forgive the sins of Christians, He does not alter the character of sin for them. In this life, sin will bring the same misery on Christians that it brings on everyone else.

Two Sides of the Coin

A woman came to a counselor I know, confessing that she was in the midst of her third extramarital affair. Her husband was ready to leave her. Since she was apparently a Christian, he began to assure her that God forgave all her sins, even third-time affairs. She began to breathe a sigh of relief as the guilt rolled off. The next week she returned, looking much happier, but the counselor was dismayed when she resisted his suggestions of again becoming faithful to her husband. Soon it was apparent that the woman wanted relief from her guilt, but did not want to turn from the sins causing the guilt. She was ready to confess her wrongdoings, but not ready to repent of them. She wanted to have her cake and eat it, too.

The counselor placed a coin on the table in front of her. Then he asked, "Try to pick one side of this coin up without the other."

"That's impossible!" she answered.

"It's the same way with God's forgiveness," he replied. "You can't pick it up without also picking up responsibility for repentance. One side of the coin is God's forgiveness. The other side is our willingness to change. You can't separate the two."

Though God forgives us, as Christians, whether or not we repent of our daily sins, I do not believe He allows us *to enjoy* our forgiveness without repentance. Because of the atonement, eternal condemnation is removed. But, if it is unrepented of, temporal penalties continue, because sin—by its nature—inflicts such damage.

The Case of David

One of the Bible's clearest examples of receiving eternal forgiveness for sin, but not escaping its logical consequences, is David. Though an outstanding king, David was an inept father and husband, who reaped the results of his weaknesses until his dying day. The Book of Deuteronomy, which David knew, warned that, if Israel selected a king, this king should not "... multiply wives for himself ..." (Deuteronomy 17:17). Though large harems were the rule for ancient kings, the Scripture wisely prohibited such a practice in Israel. The reason for large harems was not simply to gratify the king sexually, but often such marriages were ways of creating political alliances with neighboring countries. God did not want his kings to rely on marriages to beautiful pagan women for the security of Israel; the kings should trust in the Lord to protect their country. Furthermore, the multiplication of wives produced bitter family rivalries, as each wife would want to promote her own offspring to become the future king. Then, over and above these practical considerations, a permanent one-husband, one-wife relationship, as established in the Garden of Eden, was God's ideal. The king, as spiritual leader of the nation, should set the highest example.

As we study the life of David, we find that, because he had a weakness for beautiful women, he deliberately violated God's rule. First Chronicles 3:1-9 lists seven wives, nineteen sons, and one daughter. We know of one other wife (1 Samuel 18:27), so David had at least eight wives, other sons by concubines (1 Chronicles 3:9), plus other unnamed daughters. The natural consequences of this unwarranted polygamy soon erupted in his life. One of David's sons, Amnon, fell in love with his half-sister, Tamar; he attempted to seduce her and finally raped her (2 Samuel 13:1–19).

David Fails to Act

David should have administered swift justice and executed Amnon for both rape and incest, even though Amnon was his own son. But David had just seduced Bathsheba, who became his eighth wife, and murdered her husband. Guilty over his own immorality, David hesitated to execute his own son for simply following his father's example, so he did nothing. This caused another of David's sons, Absalom, to take justice into his own hands by killing Amnon. Since Absalom had murdered his brother because David failed to administer justice in the first place, David should have acknowledged his folly, forgiven his son Absalom, and tried to reunite the family. Instead Absalom was banished to a foreign country; and when he finally returned, David did not fully accept him. This led Absalom to revolt against his father and start a civil war that only ended with Absalom's death.

But the problems were not over yet. When David was old and near death, another son, Adonijah, decided he would usurp the kingship when his father died. First Kings 1:6 adds that his father, David ". . . never crossed him at any time. . . ." This headstrong son grew up without any discipline from his father, so it is no wonder that at the appropriate moment he decided to rebel and make himself king. Fortunately, his plot was foiled, and God's choice, Solomon, became king. But the result was another bloodbath: Eventually Solomon had to put Adonijah and many of his followers to death to avoid civil war in Israel.

But the story does not even end there. Solomon grew up in a family setting where his father had multiple wives and concubines, and Solomon was affected by the example. The result was that he went way beyond David, and amassed an incredible harem of seven hundred wives plus three hundred concubines. Most of David's wives were Jewish, but many of Solomon's were foreign and idolatrous, which, in his later years, led Solomon and the people into idolatry. Because of this, God judged Israel by splitting the nation in two, when Solomon's son became king. The following diagram describes the tragic consequences of David's two major sins: a weakness for attractive women and a weakness in firmly disciplining his children.

The Chain Results of Sin in David's Life

David's weakness for women leads to . . .

His marrying eight wives, seducing Bathsheba, murdering her husband. This encourages . . .

David's son, Amnon, to follow his father's example by raping Tamar, his half-sister. . . .

David, a poor disciplinarian, who was guilty over his sin with Bathsheba, refuses to punish Amnon. . . .

Absalom, Tamar's brother, avenges her rape by killing Amnon. David refuses to confess his failure to punish Amnon, instead he banishes Absalom and never fully accepts him again, even after the banishment is lifted. This encourages . . .

Absalom to revolt and start a civil war in Israel, which only ends with his death. . . .

Another son, Adonijah, whom David never disciplined, now follows Absalom's example and tries to take the crown away from Solomon, the heir apparent. . . .

Solomon kills his half-brother Adonijah, along with his followers, in another bloodbath. . . .

Solomon, affected by David's example, marries seven hundred wives and has three hundred concubines. . . .

His wives cause Solomon and Israel to turn to idolatry. . . .

God judges Israel by splitting the nation in two, when Solomon's son becomes king.

So from David's fatal flaws, of which he never seemed to repent fully, the logical consequences were one raped daughter; three dead sons, two of them killed by their brothers; a civil war; the departure of another son into idolatry; and the division of the nation. When we sow the wind, we reap the whirlwind! Though David was spiritual in other areas of his life, this did not spare him, his family, or his nation the logical consequences of his undealt-with sins. Though forgiven eternally, David endured much affliction temporally, because of his folly—folly that wasn't worth it!

No Bubble Suit

David's story illustrates how interwoven human lives are and how the mistakes of one person affect multitudes of others. We often hear such phrases as, "If I'm not hurting anyone by what I do, why can't I be free to do it?" Such people imagine that their lives exist in isolation from everyone around them. Several years ago a young boy in Houston, Texas, was found to have little or no immunity to most diseases. To enable him to survive, the National Aeronautics and Space Administration made a "bubble suit" for him, which totally enclosed him and insulated him from his environment. But we don't live in bubble suits that insulate us from affecting one another's lives. I recently encountered a case of a grandfather who committed adultery and then attempted to cover it up with a string of deceptions. After several years the whole problem came to light and resulted in a messy divorce and complex family problems. This man's actions ended up directly affecting the lives of thirty-two people, when his children, grandchildren, the family of the woman with whom he committed adultery, and various other close relatives were counted.

Many times teenagers I have talked to will try to justify taking drugs or engaging in illicit sex by saying, "It's my life; this only affects me; I can do what I want with my life." But talk to their sobbing mothers, their distraught and worried fathers, their brothers and sisters who decide to follow the same example, and you get a different picture. No man or woman is an island.

Fulfilling Our Potential

Finally, even if our sins had no immediate effect on anyone but ourselves, what about the responsibility we each have to fulfill our God-given potential in the world? Every believer in Jesus Christ has the capacity to influence people around him or her for good. We all are capable of doing something significant in the eyes of God. Suppose, in a moment of despair, Paul had said, "I won't go out to reach gentiles, start any churches, or write New Testament letters. I'll just go do my own thing and let the world go by." How impoverished our lives might now be! Suppose Peter had said, "My life is my own. I won't follow Jesus. I won't hurt anyone by remaining a fisherman. Why should I get involved with Matthew, Judas, and all these other people? I just want to be left alone."

Really we don't have the right to "do our own thing." Whether we commit open sin or simply refuse to launch out and fulfill whatever mission God has for us, we all drastically affect each other. The human race is bound together with links and ties that go on and on. We are governed by moral laws that cause our actions to affect multitudes of others for years to come, either for good or evil. In light of this, no genuine Christian should *ever* attempt to justify his waywardness with such foolish statements as, "God forgives, anyhow, so what does it matter? It's my life; if I'm not hurting others, I can do what I want." The only sensible, sane, secure way to live under God's grace is to follow God's rules.

6
THE TWO UNIONS

IF YOU CLUTCH a handful of dry sand, the tiny grains quickly leak through your fingers. You can't mold or make these grains into anything. When your family goes to the beach, your children can't even build a small fort from dry sand. They may achieve temporary success with wet sand; but, as soon as it dries, their carefully built structure blows away with the wind. Each grain seems to insist on its individuality and refuses to have anything to do with the other grains.

Damp clay is different. On our kitchen shelf is a small green and red figure of a dinosaur, which my middle daughter fashioned from damp clay and for which she won a prize. Each particle of clay clings to the other for dear life, and separating them is well-nigh impossible. You can mold clay into figures or fashion pottery from it, which, after baking, is nearly as hard as stone.

Contemporary Western society resembles the dry sand. Fierce individualism, personal rights, and doing your own thing characterize our fragmented culture. But many cultures in biblical times resembled the clay. These societies were cohesive units in which families or clans were physically and emotionally glued together in ways quite foreign to individualistic and rootless Americans.

So cohesively did many ancient peoples view themselves that the actions of parents and their offspring or the individual and the group were nearly impossible to isolate from each other. What one did, all did. What all did, one did. What parents did affected their children for generations to come. What children did reflected on their ancestors.

Solidarity Thinking

This form of group thinking, called solidarity thinking, appears often in the Bible. In Exodus 20:5 God warned the Israelites that if they turned to idolatry He would punish them ". . . unto the third and fourth generation. . ." (KJV). Would we think of punishing a person because his great-grandfather robbed a bank a hundred years ago? Yet the Bible views humans as so closely tied together that the sins of nineteenth-century ancestors may still affect their offspring today. Israel discovered this, to her dismay, when God sent her into the Babylonian captivity, partially because of the follies of King Manasseh, who had ruled eighty years earlier (2 Kings 24:1–4).

In the days of Joshua, all of Israel was defeated in battle, because the family of Achan had stolen some forbidden booty (Joshua 7). When God spoke to Joshua about Achan's rebellion, he did not say Achan had sinned, but that *Israel* had sinned (Joshua 7:11). The sins of the individual became the sins of the nation.

Though we think in highly individualistic patterns, such solidarity thinking also occurs in our own culture. For example, youths in ghettos and convicts in prisons often form into gangs. The cohesiveness of the gang provides its members with protection. If a gang member is killed, the gang takes revenge on whoever killed him, because an attack on an individual gang member is an attack on the whole gang. Yet the solidarity thinking of the modern gang is actually quite ancient. The Old Testament instituted cities of refuge, in Israel, to protect those who had caused accidental deaths from

the vengeance of the dead person's relatives. Ancient solidarity thinking dictated that the relatives must kill whoever
caused the death, for to hurt one member was to harm the
whole family.

Some Profound Insights

This seemingly strange approach to life, common to many
cultures, offers profound insight into the unity of the human
race and the effects of our lives on one another. For example,
in the nineteenth century, a young Swede immigrated to
America and eventually came to Chicago. There he met and
married a young woman of German ancestry, and eventually
I, their grandchild, was born. This couple, along with my
other grandparents and my parents, really decided that I
would be an American of Swedish and German descent.
When my Swedish grandfather crossed the Atlantic, though
I did not yet exist, I came over in him. His decisions affected
his posterity as ours will affect our posterity.

The person you have chosen or will choose to marry helps
determine the body structure, race, native intelligence, eye
color, citizenship, and so on, of your offspring for many generations. We like to think we resemble those grains of sand:
fiercely independent, determining our own fates. But, because of the unity of humankind, the decisions of parents
and grandparents automatically determine a significant portion of their descendants' destinies.

The Individual Has His Place

Of course, the Bible balances this solidarity thinking with
a proper emphasis on the individual. Ezekiel 18:20 states:
"The person who sins will die. The son will not bear the
punishment for the father's iniquity, nor will the father bear
the punishment for the son's iniquity; the righteousness of
the righteous will be upon himself, and the wickedness of the
wicked will be upon himself."

This is the other side of the coin. Though parents' decisions may strongly affect their descendants, the children still can choose to follow God or rebel and will be judged accordingly. The Jewish people of Ezekiel's time suffered captivity because of centuries of their ancestors' rebellion. Each person fatalistically said, "What's the use? My parents' sins took me from my homeland and put me in Babylon." But God told them that, despite this, they could turn to Him and live righteously, even though it was in Babylon.

This balance of unity and individuality gives us a proper perspective toward life. We see that society and the group bear responsibility for many problems. Children don't ask to be born into poverty-ridden, crime-plagued ghettos, which are often created and maintained by decisions and prejudices of our society and government. We all bear some blame for this. Yet no one who grows up in a ghetto and turns to a life of crime can legitimately say, "It's not my fault I killed and robbed and raped: Society made me do it." For human sin and failure, as well as human success and goodness, both society and the individual share responsibility.

The Two Unions

Solidarity thinking illumines a biblical doctrine often incomprehensible to Westerners: the truth of our union with Christ.

According to the Bible, two unions profoundly affect us: union with Adam and union with Christ. Because of solidarity with our first ancestor, Adam, we begin life in union with him. His rebellion in the Garden of Eden programmed us to be born with sinful natures. As we leave the womb, we are subject to sin, disease, aging, and death. Romans 5:12 states: "Therefore, just as through one man sin entered into the world, and death through sin, and so death spread to all men, because all sinned." Since we have never experienced any other state but our present fallen one, we can hardly grasp that God intended us to live differently.

Of course this raises difficult problems for the modern mind. For an educated, sophisticated twentieth-century person to believe in a literal Adam and Eve seems incredible. Yet Paul treated Adam as a historic individual (Romans 5:12–14). Luke also traces Jesus' genealogy from Adam (Luke 3:38). If Adam and Eve are not historical, where *did* sin and death originate? If God created us sinful, disease ridden, and death bound, then He becomes the author of our sin—a far greater problem than believing in Adam and Eve.

But someone else might object, "Why should Adam's decision determine my destiny? That's unfair!" The reason is that God has closely interlocked humankind. We are clay, not sand. We don't choose our parents, place of birth, sex, race, or genes. We don't even determine the color of our eyes. God simply did not will to create each of us from the dust, like Adam, place each of us in his own Garden of Eden, test each of us as He did Adam, yet have the results leave our offspring unaffected. One man and woman decided it for us all. Remember, they had everything in their favor. Their test was fair. Besides, how do I know that I would have succeeded where they failed? The Fall of the human race, through Adam and Eve, is the Bible's profound explanation of the origin of our present hang-ups and problems.

United With Christ

Just as through solidarity with one man we were ruined, so through solidarity with another man we are rescued. Romans 6:3–5 explains that at our conversion we were ". . . baptized into Christ Jesus. . . ." In the Bible the word *baptize* does not always refer to the church ritual we are familiar with; it can also mean "unite to." In 1 Corinthians 10:1, 2 Paul says, "For I do not want you to be unaware, brethren, that our fathers were all under the cloud, and all passed through the sea; and all *were baptized* into Moses in the cloud and in the sea" *(italics mine)*. The Israelis who escaped Egypt through the Red Sea "were baptized" or united to Moses. What he did, they did. He escaped Egypt, and they escaped with him.

In the same way we have been united with Jesus Christ and the benefits of His death and resurrection. Here individualistic Western thinking comes to a standstill, but solidarity thinking makes the concept clear. Just as I came over the Atlantic "in" my grandfather; just as what one gang member did involved the whole gang; just as, when Moses escaped Egypt, all Israel escaped with him: So, when Christ died to sin and arose to a new life, all believers died to sin and arose to a new life in Him.

We can grasp this better if we recall another factor: God is outside time. Time, after all, is created. Albert Einstein, the great physicist, showed that, if you could get in a rocket ship and travel at the speed of light, time would cease. Since God is the eternal Creator of time, the past and future are "right now" to Him. Ephesians 1:4 says God chose us in Christ ". . . before the foundation of the world. . . ." Before God created the world, He knew of our existence and selected us to be in Christ, because the future is ever present to Him.

Because God controls time, He could unite all believers— from the beginning to the end of history—in the benefits of Jesus' death and resurrection. One death and one resurrection at one moment of time stretch forward and backward to all believers of all ages.

Do We Become Sinless?

Romans chapter 6 further spells out the benefits of our union with Christ. Through being united with Him, Paul says we have ". . . died to sin . . ." (v. 2) and ". . . our old self was crucified . . ." (v. 6). These phrases sometimes are misinterpreted to mean that the Christian no longer sins. But, in verse 12, Paul says, ". . . do not let sin reign in your mortal body. . . ." Unless sin is present, living, and active, Paul's exhortation is needless. In Galatians 5:17 Paul stresses that the Christian continues to be a battlefield between the power of sin and the power of the Holy Spirit: "For the flesh sets its desire against the Spirit, and the Spirit against the flesh; for these are in opposition to one another, so that you may not do the things that you please."

A better interpretation of dying to sin is that we have died to the uncontested reign of sin in our lives. Sin is present in us, but no longer absolutely controls us. Once we were in the kingdom of sin. Through union with Christ, we are brought into the kingdom of God. Paul expresses this idea again in Colossians 1:13: "For He delivered us from the domain of darkness, and transferred us to the kingdom of His beloved Son." Ancient conquerors used to carry off whole populations, removing them to different locations. We have been removed from the kingdom of sin, darkness, and alienation from God, into the kingdom of righteousness, light, and peace with God. We have transferred countries.

When Israel escaped Egypt and Pharaoh in the Exodus, eventually to enter Canaan, she did not become perfect, or instantly eliminate all scars and influences of the years in Egypt. But she did escape Pharaoh's enslaving power. Before the Exodus she *had* to make his bricks; she had no choice. After the Exodus she could serve God and grow in holiness. Israel traded Pharaoh for Moses and the land of Egypt for the land of Canaan. In the same way, the Christian has traded Satan for Christ and the land of sin for the land of righteousness. He has left one country and ruler for another.

Several years ago, in Los Angeles, I met a psychiatrist who had recently escaped from Hungary. He had sharply criticized the Marxist regime there and as a result suffered continual harassment. The government was ready to imprison him. He fled by swimming across a river, as Communist soldiers shot at him. Because of his escape, my psychiatrist friend now lived in America, where he no longer needed to fear the mistreatment he had suffered in his native country. A new life was now open to him, because he had left one kingdom, where he was treated as a slave, for another, where he was at last free. He had "died" to Hungary and its problems and was now "alive" to America.

Becoming New

Not only have we died to sin, according to Romans 6, but *the old self has been crucified* (Romans 6:6). The old self is not our sinful nature. As we have just seen, the sinful nature is alive and active, setting its desires against the Spirit, so it has hardly been crucified yet. The old self (*old man* in the Greek original) is what we were in Adam; our total person as a non-Christian. The New English Bible translates the phrase, ". . . the man we once were. . . ." Before entering my union with Christ, I was joined to Adam, condemned, spiritually dead, unable to please God, headed for destruction. This is the old self. God crucified him, and I am now a new person (2 Corinthians 5:17), in union with Christ, forgiven of my sins, able to live for God, and bound for a new and wonderful destiny.

Though I am a new person in Christ, I am not yet perfect, however, for I have only experienced the first stage of my salvation. Paul himself lamented, ". . . we ourselves, having the first fruits of the Spirit, even we ourselves groan within ourselves, waiting eagerly for our adoption as sons, the redemption of our body" (Romans 8:23). The term "first fruits" describes the first part of a harvest. The Holy Spirit in us is the first part of the great harvest of our salvation. The rest will not come until the Second Coming of Christ and the resurrection of our bodies. The following chart contrasts the old man and the new man:

The Old Self (Person)	*The New Self (Person)*
1. United to Adam	1. United to Christ
2. Unforgiven	2. Forgiven
3. Only born physically	3. Also born spiritually
4. Alienated from the Holy Spirit	4. Indwelt by the Holy Spirit
5. Spiritually dead and unable to live for God	5. Spiritually alive and able to live for God
6. Headed for eternal destruction, but not there yet	6. Headed for perfect holiness, but not there yet

A Drunk Farmer

Several years ago a drunk farmer passed out in downtown Great Falls, Montana. Fortunately for him, he never returned to his motel that night, for it caught fire and burned. Authorities found a body in his room, along with his clothing and identification, so they assumed the farmer had perished in the fire.

When the farmer discovered, the next day, that he was considered dead, he was delighted. His marriage was bad; he was over his head in debt; and his future was bleak. His "death" canceled all his failures and debts, and he went out to start a new life, freed from his past. His true identity wasn't discovered until thirteen years later.

Through our union with Christ and His death, we also have broken with the person we once were and the life we once lived. Of course, we don't cast off our wives and families, refuse to pay our debts, and escape our past responsibilities, as the drunk farmer did. But we can relate in new ways to these same situations. Though in the same body, with the same personality structure, as a Christian, I have become a new person, radically severed from my old existence.

A New Self-Image

As you have read these last few pages, you have probably been saying, *This deliverance through union with Christ may be true, but why do I and other Christians experience so little of it?* The reason is that freedom from sin's reign and the benefits of union with Christ *must be counted on.* This is why, in Romans 6:11, Paul says you are to reckon (or "count on") that you are dead to sin and alive to God.

Recently the concept of self-image has attracted particular attention from the psychological community. The bestseller of a few years ago, *I'm OK, You're OK,* by psychiatrist Thomas Harris, emphasized that we should hold positive views of ourselves and others, believing that we are OK. Many psychiatrists and psychologists reject the Christian teaching that humans are sinful, since they perceive that we can hardly see ourselves as "rotten, terrible sinners" and at the same time OK.

If Christians viewed themselves as "the old self" in slavery to sin, this concern would be a just criticism. But the very truth Paul teaches in Romans 6 is that we are to view ourselves *positively.* We are to see ourselves as "dead to sin" and "alive to God." We are to count on being new persons who are capable of living new and better, though not perfect, lives. Furthermore, we are to count ourselves as new persons, not just because it makes good sense psychologically, but because it is true. In Christ, we really are new, and we really can live successful and meaningful Christian lives.

Yet when years of self-doubt and self-hate or perhaps months of depression have conditioned us not to believe, it seems impossible to come up with such positive faith. At this point counseling can often help us see why we find faith so hard to come by and help release our negative emotions, so we can become free to believe what is already true. We still must believe—from that we cannot escape. But the counselor helps us come to a point where we can exercise our own faith.

A Distraught Father

Once a distraught father came to Jesus with his demon-possessed son (Mark 9:14–29). He begged, ". . . if You can do anything, take pity on us and help us!" (v. 22). He was unsure Jesus really could help, so he said, "*If* you can help, . . . help us." Jesus challenged this basically agnostic, noncommital approach: ". . . If you can! All things are possible to him who believes" (v. 23). The man responded pitifully, but honestly, ". . . I do believe; help me in my unbelief" (v. 24). He wanted to believe, yet he admitted that doubt and unbelief hung on. The deplorable condition of his son over the years had conditioned him to expect only the worst. Perhaps his personality, like that of Doubting Thomas, was also prone to see the black side of life. Yet God honored his feeble first step into faith and healed his son.

So it is with us. We would often like a successful Christian life with only a noncommittal, agnostic attitude. We would like to leave it all in God's hands, have no faith ourselves, but just say, "Maybe He will work in my life; maybe He won't." If God doesn't work, we really didn't expect it. If He does, we're pleasantly surprised. But we make no effort to believe, take no risks, raise no hopes to be dashed.

But God will not let us escape so easily. Just as we had to actually believe, however weak and doubting our faith was, to become Christians, so we must believe the message of

Romans 6. The same Bible that says that through Christ we are rescued from sin's penalty, says that through Christ we are rescued from sin's dominion. If we know Christ, we are new people. We can be better, more healthy, more sound than we ever dreamed. We *must* see ourselves this way.

7
CLEANING UP THE CONSCIENCE

EVERY PERSON is born with a moral capacity that later develops into the conscience, but no matter how closely the Christian tries to follow the dictates of conscience, it alone will never bring him closer to God. Both this moral capacity and the conscience that develops have been contaminated by the Fall. Man is not fallen *except* for his conscience, as some have taught.

Fallen Consciences

The fallenness of the conscience shows up constantly. Paul was one example. He states in Acts 26:9: ". . . I thought to myself that I had to do many things hostile to the name of Jesus of Nazareth." His fallen, pharasaic conscience morally obligated him to persecute Christians. Jesus prophesied to the twelve that ". . . an hour is coming for everyone who kills you to think that he is offering *service to God*" (John 16:2, *italics mine*). According to Jesus, these persecutors will walk away from their bloody deeds with clear consciences, confident they obeyed God.

An equally tragic example of the fallen conscience is the punitive conscience. On a sunny California morning I stood in the shade of a tall eucalyptus tree, listened to the soft guitar music, and observed the fashionably dressed crowd assembled on the grounds of an elegant home. It was an unhappy occasion: the funeral of seventeen-year-old Susan, daughter of some friends, who had committed suicide the previous Friday. The family had gone shopping, while Susan stayed home to sunbathe. When they returned, they found her lying in a pool of blood, next to a discharged pistol—a sight that will haunt them till they die.

Contrary to what some churches teach, suicide is not an unforgivable sin. But it is one of the most tragic and certainly the most final of sinful acts. We may repent and recover from stealing, swindling, unfaithfulness, even murder. But the successful suicide obviously has closed the door on repentance and recovery in this life.

The causes of suicide vary, but an unhealthy, punitive conscience is frequently the villain. In Susan's case, apparently she was hard on herself, experienced frustrations with studies and a boyfriend, and finally felt unable to cope with just the normal stresses of life. Apparently her overdeveloped conscience constantly accused her of failure. She so despaired that she took the final, desperate step of self-destruction.

The Apostle Paul and Susan demonstrate how destructive wrongly developed consciences can be.

The concept of conscience as an unfallen, infallible guide betrays a naive and unbiblical optimism concerning human nature—an attitude that denies the depth of our depravity.

The Development of the Conscience

Psychologists feel that the conscience develops early in life, molded by a variety of personal and environmental factors. The very young child has no developed sense of right or wrong, but learns what to do and what not to do through the pleasure-pain principle. Mother tells her two-and-a-half-year-old, "Don't touch that dish, Johnny. You might break it!" A few mintues later, Johnny grabs the dish, but Mother quickly yanks it away and spanks his hands, with the reprimand, "Mommy told you not to touch the dish! You obey her!" What did Johnny learn from this? Certainly not abstract principles such as, "People should take good care of valuables," or even, "Children should obey their parents." What he learned on the surface was, "If I grab the dish, it means pain, so I won't grab it anymore." On a deeper level his childlike mind says, "When I disobey Mommy, she rejects me, so I'd better be careful about disobeying her." Actually, Mother may not be rejecting him, but he cannot yet grasp that.

When Johnny gets older, he begins to grasp morals in a more abstract sense. When he gives a black eye to little Susan, who lives next door, mother sends him to his room and scolds, "Johnny, *good boys* don't sock little girls." From this Johnny learns not only to be careful about socking Susan, but also that mother thinks some actions are good and others bad and that, if he wants Mother's love, he had better be good. Mother would probably love him, whether he was good or bad, but Johnny usually cannot understand this, no matter what she says or does.

At age ten Johnny gets another lesson in right and wrong. He hears mother tell father, "I can't stand Uncle Harry since he got so fat. I hope none of the children grow up to be fat. It's inexcusable!" Johnny now learns that it is bad to be fat, and his immature mind tells him that, if he wants Mother's love, he'd better not get fat.

Parent Tapes

These and similar experiences are called parental introjects, or parent tapes. They are the ways most children incorporate their parents' values. Parental introjects play a key role in the development of conscience. Whether or not parents realize it, they are daily fashioning healthy or unhealthy consciences in their children. Of course, other factors affect conscience formation as Johnny grows older: interaction with brothers and sisters, school, TV, friends, the mores of American culture, and Johnny's genetic makeup all play their parts. Hopefully, when Johnny reaches adulthood, he will have sifted out bad introjects from his home and environment, preserved the good, and possess sound moral judgment.

Re-educating the Conscience

Since the conscience is sinful and frequently develops in unhealthy directions, the Christian must re-educate and renew his, to make it function properly. Paul speaks of renewing the mind, in Romans 12:2, which probably includes renewing the conscience, since, in Scripture, the mind is often the center of moral judgment. I would like to propose three steps for renewing the conscience: first, adjust the conscience to biblical standards; second, adjust the conscience to biblical feelings; third, adjust the conscience to the tension between the real and ideal.

Adjusting the conscience to biblical standards can be difficult. The standards of conscience are its moral rules: what it sees as right and wrong. What has been fed into the conscience usually determines its moral standards. As with a computer, this can become "garbage in, garbage out." Paul's non-Christian conscience was fed pharisaism, and out came persecution of Christians. The Nazi conscience was fed anti-Semitism, and out came Auschwitz. When we become Christians, we should begin to pass our standards through the biblical filter, so we can come out with the biblical viewpoint. Biblical absolutes must supplant our life-long prejudices and distorted values. Often this means the standards of conscience must become *more strict*.

Moral relativism and growing hedonism characterize America. Some who claim to be Christians try to rationalize sex outside marriage, heavy drinking, homosexuality, X-rated movies, subscriptions to *Playboy,* manipulation, deception, and hedonistic materialism. They ridicule those who condemn their practices, calling them legalists, while they justify their permissive and undisciplined life-styles as being "under grace." The Corinthian church followed this pattern in the New Testament. Such persons are on a collision course with Scripture's exacting moral demands. The Bible *never* pictures marital faithfulness as legalism! The Christian life demands morality, discipline, and sacrifice. Christians who refuse to internalize such biblical standards soon discover that they are of limited use to God and that self-caused pain and suffering are their frequent lot, because they reap what they sow. Unfortunately, an overly permissive Christianity characterizes too many churches—in some cases, even at leadership levels.

In some tragic cases, professing Christians lack any conscience at all. Psychologists call these persons *psychopathic personalities.* Many psychopaths are neither inhuman tyrants nor fugitives from justice. They may even be law-abiding citizens.

Several years ago I tried to help a midwestern minister and his wife patch up their disintegrating marriage. I failed, and she divorced him. He protested that he had always been faithful to her, so she lacked any biblical ground for divorce. I later discovered that he had lied and gone from one sexual escapade to another. When I confronted him with his misdeed, I could not detect that he felt any guilt. Through clever manipulation, he remains, to this day, the senior minister of a church, despite a double life and repeated attempts to remove him from his position. Unfortunately, such Elmer Gantrys have always plagued the church and always will.

Those with psychopathic tendencies must face their need to submit to biblical standards and surrender their proneness to live in moral anarchy.

The standards for other Christians, however, must become more relaxed. Some of the early Roman Christians had consciences that assured them that all Christians should be vegetarians. Paul called these Romans "weak in faith" and encouraged them not to condemn their meat-eating brethren (Romans 14:1–3). Scripture grants us freedom to be vegetarians, but not to make our diets a moral issue. We must not impose pharisaic rules on the church—rules that come from our fallen consciences, rather than from Scripture.

As a young Christian in the 1950s, I received much of my Christian growth from a group that, good as it was, tended to be overly strict. I recall attending a conference, then, where the speaker emphasized that Christian women should avoid wearing makeup, because it was "worldly." I noticed that the teenage girls who worked as waitresses at the conference, unlike other teenagers in those years, wore no makeup. Ironically, when the sixties' youth rebellion struck, radical hippie women began to look like what the speaker had implied was "Christian," as they grew long hair, wore old-fashioned dresses, metal-rimmed glasses, and no makeup or jewelry, in rebellion against the establishment. Little did these radical young women realize that some conservative Christian schools had been encouraging some of the hippie fashions for several generations!

The problem with this speaker's approach was that he believed Christians should look different on the outside, while the biblical view is that they are different on the inside. Though New Testament Christians avoided sensual and extravagant dress styles, their appearance generally resembled that of others in their culture. The New Testament never implies that Jesus' dress was different from the ordinary fashions of His day. Their lives, not their clothing, distinguished the early Christians.

When such external standards are fed into the conscience, another garbage-in, garbage-out situation results. The externalism, asceticism, and legalism that were fed in cause self-righteousness, hypocrisy, and false guilt to come out. The cure is again to filter standards and prejudices of your background through Scripture. If your background was overly strict and legalistic, scriptural standards will actually loosen you up in some areas, but without moral compromise.

Most of us are somewhere between the extreme examples of being too loose or too strict. One of our most complex tasks is to develop the healthy conscience God wants us to have rather than the conscience someone else wants us to have.

Getting the Right Feeling

The second step in renewing the conscience is to adjust it to what I call biblical feelings. Our consciences not only absorb false behavioral standards from our early environment, but false feelings about ourselves, as well. One of the reasons for this is the all-importance of our parents, in our early lives. As small children, we depend on our parents for food, shelter, love, and guidance. They are like all-knowing, all-powerful gods in our lives, holding the keys to our survival. As immature little persons, we are unable to evaluate maturely and objectively the feelings they communicate to us about ourselves.

For example, one day, little Johnny's father may come home from work, angry and frustrated. Maybe he stopped at a bar on the way. As he walks up the frontsteps, he trips over Johnny's wagon and shouts, "Johnny! Put that wagon in the garage, as I told you, or I'll give it away. Can't you ever learn to do anything?" Perhaps Johnny's father frequently drinks too much and loses his temper. But Johnny is too immature to see this as his father's problem. Johnny feels his very existence depends on keeping in the good graces of his all-powerful father. So, instead of thinking, *There's something wrong with Daddy. He shouldn't drink so much,* Johnny may reason instead, *There's something wrong with* me. *I'd better work harder to keep him happy. If I don't, he won't love me anymore.* The result may be that Johnny's conscience, filled with father's parent tapes, becomes tyrannical. It's always on his back, just like his father. He's always working to please it, but never can. He develops a deep sense of worthlessness and, as an adult, finds the love and forgiveness of God difficult to accept. Johnny's conscience absorbs far more than simply the standards of his father: "You should put the wagon away when I tell you." It absorbs his father's feelings of anger and rejection and internalizes them into his conscience. The conscience now becomes like Johnny's rejecting father carried around inside him for life.

But the problem may become even worse. Though Johnny's father may have had a drinking problem and at times taken out frustrations on his son, at other times, he was probably kind and loving toward Johnny. But because of his childish fears, Johnny will tend to amplify his father's rejection beyond what it was. As he plays father's rejecting-parent tapes, he turns up the volume five times, on a multiple speaker system! This is one reason why we tend to feel insecure underneath, no matter how we were loved. As psychologist Bruce Narramore has shown, as small children, we usually exaggerated parental rejections and expectations beyond what they were. So instead of carrying around, in his conscience, a father who rejects him sometimes and accepts him other times, Johnny will carry around a father who severely rejects him all the time.

The Law and the Conscience

To those who have such punitive consciences, biblical teachings about Law and grace are especially important. We have already noted that *grace* is God's unearned acceptance. The Bible often uses the term *law*, on the other hand, to speak of earned acceptance. Paul writes in Galatians 3:12, ". . . the Law is not of faith; on the contrary, 'He who practices them [the standards of the Law] shall live by them.' " In Romans 10:5 he repeats the same thought: "For Moses writes that the man who practices the righteousness which is based on law shall live by that righteousness." The Law requires works and obedience. If we obey it, the Law rewards us; if we violate it, the Law punishes us.

Because the Law and the punitive conscience operate by works, they are drawn to each other like magnets. Christians with punitive consciences readily internalize the Law and become overloaded with guilt, because they are not doing all the Law demands. When they fail, conscience, made more punitive by the Law, lashes them. The Christian under Law is often more miserable than if he were not a Christian at all. One day I sat at lunch with a youth minister. He told me, in effect, "Bill, I've had it! I faithfully carry on the youth ministry in my church. We have a growing youth group; the church likes what I do. But, inside, I'm miserable. When I get together with other youth ministers, I find myself in a constant spirit of competition. I want to outdo them, to do a better job than they do, to have more kids in my program than they do. The youth group has merely become a means for me to achieve my own success. I feel I've never done enough. Whenever I go to bed at night, my conscience, like some demanding tyrant, keeps bugging me to do more. Always more, more, more."

He was *under Law*. He knew that Christ had died for him,

and that he was going to heaven. But, in this life, his whole success was based on works. The more works, the more God loved him and his conscience praised him. The fewer works, the less God loved him and the more his conscience punished him.

Too Many Rules

Since those with punitive consciences want to appease both their consciences and God through works, they naturally search for external, keepable behavior patterns, frequently in the form of rules. Often these people are obsessive-compulsive types, with exact rules for use of their time, personal devotions, physical exercise, giving money, raising children—even exact rules as to when they can relax and what they must do when they "relax." Rules and guidelines are necessary, if we are to lead disciplined lives. I set aside a regular time for jogging and donate a certain percentage of my income to the church. But, when most of our lives are rule dominated, we are obviously insecure underneath and are attempting, through rules, to avoid anxieties and placate angry consciences.

I once counseled a young athlete whose whole life was under such rules. When doing his studies, he would read his college textbook fifty minutes and a Christian devotional book for ten minutes. He would allow so many minutes per day for conversations, so many for recreation, so many for a nap, and so on. He rigidly structured his day into carefully planned time segments that were all but unalterable. I felt as if I were relating to an efficient, but lifeless, computer, rather than a flesh-and-blood person! Jesus was disciplined, but He never structured His life so rigidly.

On another occasion I counseled a young woman who was so into jogging that it had become an obsession around which her whole life revolved. If, for some reason, she missed a workout, an almost uncontrollable terror would grip her.

Jogging helped her avoid deep anxieties and placate an angry conscience, but not in a healthy way.

Too Many Seminars?

On a lesser level many church members overload themselves with rules from the proliferating number of how-to seminars and books so popular in America. Many of these seminars and books have been helpful to me. But they run the danger of straitjacketing the Christian life into a few inflexible techniques. The person with a punitive conscience will often come away from the latest marriage, child-raising, time-management, or evangelism seminar with a new set of rules he and the family must rigidly obey, making their Christian lives increasingly mechanical and inflexible.

Unfortunately, such people fail to realize that the Bible offers no rigid set of techniques. The technique approach to living is largely a product of the Western business mentality, which in turn has been influenced by behavioristic psychology. The biblical approach is broad and flexible, adaptable to every kind of personality and culture. It resembles a men's clothing store, with styles, colors, and sizes for every kind of customer. The technique approach, which offers to simplify life into a few narrow how-tos, is like a clothing store that sells only size forty-two-long brown suits which all customers must fit into, because these suits look good on the owner.

Curing the Punitive Conscience

Unfortunately, the punitive conscience knows no easy cure, though it is comforting to learn that such great Christians as Saint Augustine, Martin Luther, and John Bunyan were afflicted with punitive consciences, yet were highly successful. Basically, the person with the punitive conscience must work on replacing the amplified rejecting-parent tapes of early childhood with divine parent tapes. The Scriptures picture God as an ideal parent, who would naturally provide the perfect parental introjects for our Christian consciences. Hebrews 12:5 states "My son, do not regard lightly the discipline of the Lord, Nor faint when you are reproved by Him; for those whom the Lord loves He disciplines, and He scourges every son whom He receives."

The Greek word used here for "discipline," *paideuo*, means "to train," as in training a child. Such training includes positive commands and examples, as well as negative experiences such as prohibitions or corrections. The scourge was a brutal instrument used to punish criminals, but scholars feel that the word is far more mild here, meaning "to chastise." Scourging is parallel to spanking a child, the negative side of discipline. As a good parent, God both commends our good actions and corrects, or spanks, us for bad behavior, yet always in love. "... *Whom the Lord loves He disciplines....*" A conscience reflecting the voice of God would thus give us a good feeling when we obey God, and seek to correct us in love when we disobey, yet it would always treat us out of love and grace.

But the conscience which judicially punishes us and tells us we are worthless and unlovable is denying the atoning work of Christ, opposing God, and illegitimately using the law on us. Romans 8:1 states, "There is therefore now *no condemnation* for those who are in Christ Jesus" *(italics mine)*. Romans 3:28 states we are made acceptable to God, or justified, "... by faith *apart from* works of the Law" *(italics mine)*. If my conscience punishes me when God does not, then conscience is exalting itself over God. John seems to be putting such a conscience in its place when he says, "We shall know by this that we are of the truth, and shall assure our heart [conscience] before Him, in whatever our heart [conscience] condemns us; for God is greater than our heart [conscience], and knows all things" (1 John 3:19, 20). The force of the verse is that, even if conscience condemns, God is *greater* than conscience, knows we are forgiven, and does not condemn. If it is a choice between the condemning voice of a sinful conscience and the loving voice of a holy God, we must choose the voice of God!

The healthy conscience carries the voice of God to us. But, if we listen carefully, we find our consciences often don't carry God's voice at all. That nagging, berating, and fault-finding conscience is not bringing us the voice of God, but the exaggerated and amplified voices of our fathers and mothers, which we heard when we were small children.

God wants us to begin turning off those distorted and fallen parent tapes and start turning on parent tapes for Him. He corrects us in love. He encourages us to repent. He holds true biblical standards before us. But He does not berate, attack, and condemn us. He is not the parent we can never please. He is the ideal parent—both loving and firm—that we all have secretly longed for. A conscience carrying His voice produces balanced, healthy, happy people.

The Real and the Ideal

The final step in renewing the conscience is to teach it to live with the tension between the real and the ideal. The Christian finds, in the Bible, flawless and ideal standards for his behavior. God does not lower His righteousness because we cannot match up to it. Yet Scripture never teaches we will achieve these ideals *in this life.* After being a Christian for probably more than sixty years, John wrote, "If we say that we have no sin, we are deceiving ourselves . . ." (1 John 1:8). If, after sixty years, one of the twelve apostles still was sinful, shall we do better?

Perhaps what helps us here is to remember that, though we are sinful, fallen, and make mistakes, we are forgiven and can still be useful to God. When I drink water from my kitchen faucet, I am not drinking perfect water. It contains impurities, chemicals, and bacteria. Though it is *imperfect,* however, it is still *useful* and quenches my thirst. A champion tennis player does not win tournaments through playing perfect tennis. He occasionally loses games, misses shots, and fails to put his opponent away, when he has the chance. Though his game is far from perfect, he still wins tournaments and walks off with prize money.

If my conscience demands from me a perfect, mistake-free, continually successful Christian life, rather than a useful and fruitful one, its requirements are above God's. Paul, Augustine, Luther, John Wesley, and other great Christians were far from perfect, yet their lives were abundantly fruitful. Because we possess a God-given longing for perfection, we expect perfection of ourselves and others here and now, forgetting that God perfects us according to His timetable, not ours. A fruit of the Spirit is patience.

The mature Christian patiently endures his imperfection, longing for the day when he can cast it off, rather than insisting that God cause him to arrive, spiritually, in the next five minutes.

Hopefully, if we follow the three steps I have just suggested, we can clean up our bad consciences and make them helpful servants rather than hard taskmasters.

8
THE REAL YOU

SEVERAL YEARS AGO, plastic surgeon Maxwell Maltz wrote
the best-seller *Psycho-Cybernetics,* to help people improve their
self-images. Dr. Maltz began to study self-image, because he
noticed his patients' physical appearances could improve
radically, through surgery, while their self-images remained
glued to their former looks. Once he made an ugly woman
beautiful by removing a disfiguring hump from her nose, yet
she remained self-conscious, refused to look others in the eye,
and retreated to the nearest corner whenever she could. Her
mirror told her she had a new nose, but her self-image told
her the hump remained, so she kept behaving like the ugly
duckling.

Recently a powerful Hollywood executive embezzled forty
thousand dollars, though he annually earned over seven
times that much and did not need the money. After twenty-
one months of therapy, he acknowledged that he stole the
money to punish himself for rising to the top. His self-image
told him he was unworthy of success; so, when success came,
he felt obligated to fail.

Self-image is how we see ourselves. We may feel good or
bad about ourselves, see ourselves as winners or losers, worthy or unworthy, competent or helpless, attractive or repul-
sive; we may think people are for or against us: These
thoughts and feelings make up the self-image. We will tend
to behave consistently with our self-images, even though our

87

actions fly in the face of reality. Many times, to change behavior patterns, we have to change the self-image that produces them. Perhaps the biblical writer had self-image in
mind when he penned of man, ". . . as he thinketh in his
heart, so is he . . ." (Proverbs 23:7 KJV).

Discipline and Self-Image

Like the conscience, self-image develops early in life, from
interaction with our environment. Many psychiatrists used
to teach that parental permissiveness produced a good self-
image. They theorized that little discipline, few rules, and
immediate gratification of most desires would decrease children's inner conflicts and cause them to view themselves positively. But a study by Stanley Coopersmith, *The Antecedents
of Self-Esteem,* shows that parents who set consistent rules and
discipline their children firmly, regularly, and lovingly tend
to raise emotionally healthy offspring with good self-images.
Discipline prepares a child for the real world, where frequently he cannot do whatever he wants whenever he wants
to. Discipline gives the child the secure feeling that his parents care about him, will set limits for him, and will make
the decisions that he is too immature to make for himself.
But, unless love accompanies such discipline, the child may
feel rejected and worthless. Plenty of love and plenty of discipline are the fertile soils that usually grow healthy self-
images. The Bible taught this for centuries, though it has
only recently dawned on some experts!

Yet parents don't have the last word. Through using correct child-praising techniques parents may influence, but
cannot guarantee, their children's outcome. They can provide an environment conducive to good results and hope for
the best. This normally works. But sometimes children from
good homes end up with bad self-images and vice versa. The

Garden of Eden was Adam and Eve's home, and God was their parent, yet they were free to fail, and they did.

Our Many Selves

The self-image, of course, is only part of your total self. The total self is so complex that we might understand it better by dividing it into different selves. These are not different personalities, but facets of one total self. We might call one facet the *imagined self,* since this is who you think you are. But you also have a *projected self,* which is who you want others to think you are. Then you have an *ideal self,* closely tied to conscience, which is who you think you should be. Finally you have a *true self,* which is who you are in God's eyes. We could subdivide these selves further and label them more precisely, if we were to become more technical.

Originally these selves harmonized with each other. Before his fall, Adam's imagined, projected, ideal, and true selves agreed that he was an unfallen person, created in God's image. What happened when he rebelled against God? His ideal self retained the memory of his unfallen state and reminded Adam he should still be sinless. But since his true self was fallen, it clashed with this ideal self, producing guilt. What Adam should have been (the ideal self) and what he was (the true self) opposed each other.

The Fall also distorted Adam's projected self. Adam and Eve feared revealing to each other and God that they were rebellious, fallen humans. They hid from each other by donning fig leaves, and attempted to hide from God by concealing themselves among the trees. Adam and Eve were no longer trusting or transparent. Their projected selves worked to hide their true identities from each other, outsiders, and God, and—if necessary—to deceive others about who they were.

Adam's imagined self apparently realized he was fallen, but wanted to blame others for his problem. When God confronted Adam over his sin, Adam accused Eve—and, ultimately, God—of engineering his predicament. So Adam's true self was fallen; his ideal self reminded him he should have been unfallen; his projected self tried to hide his fallenness; and his imagined self tried to blame others for it. We might diagram Adam's selves before and after the Fall this way:

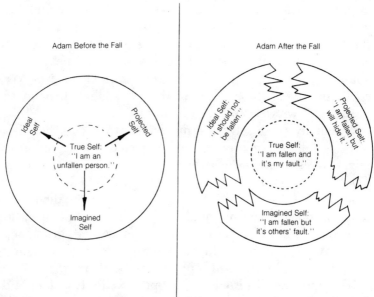

Adam Before the Fall

Ideal Self

Projected Self

True Self: "I am an unfallen person."

Imagined Self

Adam After the Fall

Ideal Self: "I should not be fallen."

Projected Self: "I am fallen but will hide it."

True Self: "I am fallen and it's my fault."

Imagined Self: "I am fallen but it's others' fault."

Recovering From the Fall

Since Adam's fractured selves sometimes opposed or deceived one another, he became the complex, sometimes irrational, sinful being who no longer even understood his own soul. Obviously, this describes us all. But when we become Christians, our divided selves should begin to reunite, as we grasp appropriate biblical truths about self-unity. Fundamental to reuniting the selves is understanding who the true self now is, who you are in God's eyes. The Bible has much to say about this.

Though still fallen, our true self remains in God's image and possesses nobility, simply because we are human beings. God told Noah, "Whoever sheds man's blood, By man his blood shall be shed, *For in the image of God He made man"* (Genesis 9:6 *italics mine).* This shows sinful man is still an image bearer, as does a parallel passage, about the tongue, in James 3:9, 10: "With it [the tongue] we bless our Lord and Father; and with it we curse men, who have been *made in the likeness of God. . . .* My brethren, these things ought not to be this way" *(italics mine).* Jesus frequently emphasized the value of human image bearers, in contrast to dumb animals. He rebuked the Pharisees for kindness to sheep, but not people, with a cutting, "Of *how much more value* then is a man than a sheep! . . ." (Matthew 12:12, *italics mine).*

But being image bearers does not diminish our sinfulness. Paul declares: ". . . we have already charged that both Jews and Greeks [gentiles] are all under sin; as it is written, 'There is none righteous, not even one . . . . there is none who does good, there is not even one.' . . . for all have sinned and fall short of the glory of God" (Romans 3:9, 10, 12, 23). The threat of atomic war, the peril of population explosion, the specter of world famine, and the squandering of natural resources demonstrate on an international level our inability to manage ourselves, while selfishness, manipulation, deception, unfaithfulness, and other sins reveal on a personal level that we have descended a long way from Eden. The comic-strip character said it right: "We have met the enemy, and he is us."

A Realistic View

If we view ourselves realistically, we must believe we are *both* noble and fallen: image bearers and sinners. Several years ago in Athens, Greece, I viewed the Parthenon, an ancient Greek temple finished by 432 B.C., it is one of the most perfect buildings ever constructed. Unfortunately, in 1687 Turkish authorities stored gunpowder in it, which blew up during a siege. The Parthenon today is *both* magnificent and ruined. Almost every stone in it declares the genius of ancient Greece. Yet the roof is gone, portions are collapsed, and rubble lies scattered about.

Similarly, we are a magnificent ruins. But when we see ourselves as only magnificent or only ruins, we are in trouble. Many biblical truths are two sided: that God is one, yet three persons; that God controls all, yet humans make significant choices; that God works in us, yet we also work; that faith alone saves, yet faith that saves is not alone. When we stress only one side of such truths, we build one-walled houses. Many secular psychologists see man as being basically OK. Some secularists even teach we can prosper as a nation with almost no government, learn in schools with almost no requirements, and achieve emotional health in homes with almost no parental discipline. On the other hand, some in the church—as well as some modern writers and artists—see humans as being so corrupt that they are no longer image bearers. So many Christian books, hymns, and sermons paint this picture, that critics have rightly dubbed it "worm theology." Like tightrope walkers, we must balance our poles evenly and avoid one-sided theologies.

The Christian Dimension

All humans are both noble and fallen, but the Christian has added dimensions. First, he experiences God's love and forgiveness. Paul marvels in Ephesians 2:4 at God's ". . . great love with which He loved us" and rejoices in Ephesians 1:7 that ". . . we have redemption through His blood, the forgiveness of our trespasses. . . ." Second, the believer is a new creation and the dwelling place of the Holy Spirit. Paul tells the Corinthians that in Christ they are new creatures (2 Corinthians 5:17) and that each has a body that ". . . is a temple of the Holy Spirit . . ." (1 Corinthians 6:19). This makes the Christian more complex than the non-Christian. His true self now contains a renewed spiritual self that coexists with the sinful, rebellious self.

For a non-Christian to assess himself accurately, he must realize he is estranged from God. In fact, when he begins to face this truth, he usually becomes a Christian. For a Christian to assess himself accurately, he must believe he is forgiven, loved, a new creation, and indwelt by God's Holy Spirit. These are not characteristics that result from dedicated living. They are rather what *cause* dedicated living.

But there is more. The general truths above describe all Christians. Beyond them are particular truths about particular Christians. For example, God gives different spiritual gifts to believers. Paul writes ". . . since we have gifts that differ according to the grace given to us, let each exercise them accordingly . . ." (Romans 12:6). Along with our gifts, evidently, go certain personality styles. The Christian gifted as an erudite scholar, who spends endless hours studying in a quiet library, will usually be more contemplative and introverted. The Christian with the gift of evangelism, who frequently encounters people and presents Christ to them, will usually be more active and extroverted. One with a gift of helping, who remains in the background and quietly keeps the church books will usually have a personality quite different from the eloquent Bible teacher who enthralls thousands each Sunday. Even those with similar gifts, such as the twelve apostles, possessed differing personality styles. Peter was impulsive and action oriented, while John was mystical and ethereal. In addition to personality styles, our genetic makeups differ. We are male or female, tall or short, slightly or heavily built, attractive or average in appearance.

Knowing Yourself

All these ingredients make up the true self. We are noble; sinful; loved; forgiven; becoming new; temples of God's Spirit; differently gifted with different personalities, genetic makeups, and appearances. If one's *true* self is the above, then his *imagined* self, *projected* self, and his *ideal* self should be consistent with it. Christian growth means reuniting the selves splintered apart by the Fall. Psychologists call this self-unity *congruence*.

Congruence is fundamental to mental health. People whose outward behavior contradicts their inner beings, whose self-images contradict what they are, whose ideas contradict what they can ever become, entangle themselves in webs of neurotic deceit. In contrast, the Bible commends truthfulness and genuineness. God is a "... God of truth ..." (Isaiah 65:16), who "... cannot lie ..." (Titus 1:2), Jesus claimed "... I am ... the truth ..." (John 14:6), the Holy Spirit is "... the Spirit of truth ..." (John 14:17). Paul commands us to "... speak truth ..." (Ephesians 4:25). John tells us to love "... in deed and truth" (1 John 3:18). On the other hand, Satan is "... a liar, and the father of lies" (John 8:44).

We trust God, because He is congruent. Who He really is, who He thinks He is, who He tells us He is and who He ought to be are the same. Jesus was congruent. He was God incarnate. Though He was God incarnate and projected himself as God incarnate, He did not deceive, manipulate, or play games.

The Congruent Christian

The congruent Christian forms an imagined, projected, and ideal self consistent with his true self. Since his true self is image bearer and sinner, contains a rebellious and new self, possesses certain gifts, a unique genetic makeup, and a distinct personality style, his imagined and projected self reflect this. He sees himself as a certain kind of person and reveals this same kind of person to others. If he is an introvert, he may seek to smooth the rough edges of this personality style, but will not try to become an extrovert. If he is male, he will refuse to assume a female role (as some homosexuals do). If he is fifty, he will not behave as if he were twenty. Romans 12:3 commands us to think about ourselves with "... sound judgment ...," which means to view ourselves as we are, rather than to imagine a self that doesn't exist.

The congruent Christian's ideal self, of necessity, experiences some tension with his other selves, because he has not yet arrived at the goal of biblical perfection. But he claims forgiveness and senses progress. Furthermore, he knows his ideal self reflects God's will *for him,* not for someone else. Peter once questioned Jesus about God's will for fellow-apostle John. "... Lord, and what about this man?" he said (John 21:21). Jesus replied that this was none of Peter's business. John does not copy Peter, or vice versa. Because others have followed certain paths and succeeded does not mean we should. God has an individual will for each person.

Paul was a congruent Christian. He knew he was forgiven for grievous sins, so he did not wallow in self-pity. He knew he was an apostle to the gentiles, so he altered his Jewish life-style. He knew he possessed a gift of celibacy, so he did not seek marriage. He knew he possessed leadership gifts, so he did not seek to be a follower. Paul was true to himself.

Games We Play

Unfortunately, many of us are not so congruent. I once briefly attended a church where the minister projected himself as a General Patton in the pulpit. He was authoritarian, domineering, outwardly dead sure of himself. I happened to run into him one day, in a coffee shop, and in the course of conversation told him I disagreed with his interpretation of a particular verse of Scripture. Immediately he lost his bluster and became uncertain, almost apologetic. I could see that behind the projected self of an almighty general in God's army was a frightened little boy. He projected himself as dogmatic and dominating, to conceal the uncertainty and frailty in his self-image. Parallel to this, I have a friend who is outwardly autocratic and self-assured, but falls apart when confronted with even minor faults. The weaker he feels, the stronger he tries to project himself. Actually the military-style minister and my friend are secure and able to do God's will in their true selves. But because fear and weakness haunt their self-images, they try to compensate with dominating and authoritarian personality styles. Their warring selves get in each other's way, blocking their potential for God.

To become congruent, they would have to admit they felt weak and fearful, realize that God's love and strength make such fear unnecessary, and project confident but no-longer arrogant selves to the outside world.

What Should We Be?

Another problem often surfaces in our ideal selves. The ideal self should reflect what God wants us to become. This means final perfection in heaven and achieving our maximum potential on earth, given our genetic makeups, gifts, personality styles, and circumstances. Yet often our ideal selves dictate that we should become what others expect, rather than what God expects. God does not strengthen the true self to become what He does not want; so, if we mistakenly pursue such a course, we create our own unnecessary frustrations.

In *Your Spiritual Gifts Can Help Your Church Grow,* church-growth expert C. Peter Wagner discusses such a problem. He claims that Christians with remarkable gifts of faith, leadership, evangelism, and so on, will often state they lack any special gifts and emphasize that *any Christian* could do what they do, if he or she would just trust God. Wagner calls this *gift projection,* because the Christian with an outstanding gift is sincerely, but mistakenly, trying to make every member of the body practice his gift.

Gift projection is the same as saying anyone can run a world-record mile, if he just trains; anyone can be a famous musician, if he just practices; or anyone can win a Nobel Prize, if he just studies. It overlooks that hard work cannot replace talent and gift. Paul says ". . . we have gifts that *differ* . . ." (Romans 12:6, *italics mine*), and adds in another place, "All are not apostles, are they? All are not prophets, are they? All are not teachers, are they? . . . All do not speak with tongues, do they? . . ." (1 Corinthians 12:29, 30).

I once talked with an airplane pilot employed by a Christian organization. He was a skilled pilot and mechanic, but became frustrated because his organization wanted him to do public-relations work, fund raising, and evangelism, which were not part of his original job description. He was told that, if he was Spirit-filled and trusted God, he would succeed, for Paul taught, "I can do all things through Him who strengthens me" (Philippians 4:13).

Such teaching, all too common in Christianity, puts round pegs in square holes and promotes many Christians to their levels of incompetence. Our ideal selves should reflect God's goals for us—which will be consistent with the gifts and personalities He bestowed upon us—rather than the goals friends, churches, families, or Christian organizations set up for us.

Avoiding Self-Centeredness

Another problem with our many selves is self-centeredness. Many people twist the above truths to defend self-centered behavior. For example, some Christians abuse biblical teaching on spiritual gifts, to keep from obeying God. They may refuse to tell anyone about Christ, because they lack the gift of evangelism; or refuse to organize their lives, because they lack the gift of administration; or refuse to believe biblical promises, because they don't have the gift of faith. Such attitudes are inexcusable. Others abuse the biblical emphasis that we have different personalities and makeups: "This is the way I was born; don't expect me to change," they respond, when confronted with sin.

We can avoid such justifications of selfish behavior, if we understand our true selves more deeply. As stated earlier, the true self contains two selves: a renewed self and a rebellious self. The Bible calls the rebellious self "the flesh." Theologians call it "indwelling sin." In Romans 7:17 Paul makes the rebellious self responsible for his sins: "So now, no longer am I the one doing it, but sin [the rebellious self] which indwells me." Paul sees the rebellious self as distinct from "I." He says sin indwells me, but is not the same as me. Romans 7 pictures the true Paul ("I") as wanting to obey God, but the rebellious self as an alien force that overwhelms him.

We must view the rebellious self as an unnatural part of each of us, as Paul does in Romans 7. God designed humankind in His image, to reflect His glory. As an exquisite painting mirrors the genius of its artist, so we were to reflect Almighty God's creative genius. Through the Fall, the image became blemished; but, through coming to Christ, the image is being restored. God did not make humans sinners; sin is foreign to them. "To err is human" wrongly suggests that to be human means to be fallen. Sin is to humans as sand is to the gas tank, salt is to the sugar bowl, or viruses are to the bloodstream. We were made to live without it. To be human, in the best sense, is to be sinless.

Early in our marriage, my wife and I and our small child moved from California to Texas. Since our possessions and funds were limited, we stuffed our belongings into a U-Haul trailer, attached it to our small station wagon, and began the trek to our new home. The heavy trailer made driving difficult and gas mileage terrible. We slowly struggled up hills and crept cautiously down them, fearing that either our radiator or our brakes would overheat. We were relieved to arrive at our new home and drop off the trailer, so our car could again perform normally. The trailer is like the rebellious self: It was not a natural part of the car, nor is sin a natural part of us. The trailer bogged the car down, as sin does us. The trailer was temporary, and its removal restored the car to normal operations. Sin is temporary, and its elimination releases us to become normal humans.

Being True to Yourself

For the Christian to be true to himself, he must be true to the renewed, not the rebellious, self. The renewed self is the permanent and real person. The rebellious self is a temporary abnormality, an unwanted alien. You can test this in your own experience. When you sin and follow the rebellious self, how do you often feel afterwards? You are fragmented and at war with yourself! How do you feel when you follow the renewed self and obey God? You are whole and at peace with yourself! This is because being righteous is being true to who you really are: a renewed person headed for heaven. Being evil is opposing who you really are, which is why you feel divided and estranged over sin.

The Old Testament character Lot, Abraham's nephew, powerfully illustrates a believer who is untrue to himself. Though Lot trusted in God, the prosperity of the evil city of Sodom enticed him away from the Lord. After Lot settled down in Sodom, 2 Peter 2:7, 8 says he became ". . . oppressed by the sensual conduct of unprincipled men (for by what he saw and heard that righteous man, while living among them, felt his righteous soul tormented day after day with their lawless deeds).'' Sodom "oppressed" and "tormented" Lot. Why? Because he was *too good* for the place! Sodom's outrageous sins failed to bother its unbelieving citizenry. Its evil deeds were normal behavior, so far as they were concerned. But for Lot to live in the midst of such moral darkness was to be untrue to himself. Lot was trying to fit in where he never could. No wonder he felt fragmented and miserable!

One evening, over dinner, I talked with a young real-estate executive whose life paralleled Lot's in some areas. He was a Christian; but, like Lot, he was compromising his true self. He was sexually involved with his girl friend, rarely read his Bible, and only occasionally attended Christian gatherings. I looked him straight in the eye and said, "Steve, you are denying who you really are. In the depth of your soul, you're a Christian. You'll never find fulfillment until you come out of the closet and live what you believe underneath." Paul said much the same to the Ephesians: ". . . now you are light in the Lord; walk as children of light" (Ephesians 5:8). In other words, *be* what you *are;* don't masquerade as an unbeliever!

Instead of catering to your rebellious self, following its promptings, and excusing yourself with "That's just the way I am, I can't help it," you should oppose the rebellious self and say, "That's *not* the way I am!" The rebellious self is the outsider you can do without, the temporary blemish, the U-Haul trailer to be dropped off.

The "real you," which will go on forever, which God is rebuilding and renewing—that is where your loyalty belongs. Christian, be true to yourself!

9
SERVING THE "ME GENERATION"

FROM GREEK MYTHOLOGY comes the tale of Narcissus, a handsome but conceited youth who fell in love with his own reflection in a pool and kept staring at it, until he wasted away and died. The gods then transformed him into the yellow and white flower that now bears his name. From this story we get the term *narcissism* to describe neurotically self-centered people. All of us are self-centered, but the narcissist is so intensely selfish that he becomes a problem to society.

Unfortunately, such neurotic selfishness, once characteristic of a minority, now threatens to engulf the whole population. We are becoming such a nation of narcissists that popular writers call this the "me generation."

A trip to my neighborhood bookstore reveals that this description fits. On the display racks I discover titles like *Looking Out for No. 1, Getting Yours, Own Your Own Life, Pulling Your Own Strings, How to Get the Upper Hand, How to Make Things Go Your Way,* and *The Art of Selfishness.* One book offers its own version of the golden rule, a chapter entitled: "Teach others how you want to be treated." Another extensively discusses "the principles of pleasure," while another warns against "thinking of others first."

At the newsstand it's no better. A new women's magazine appropriately entitled *Self* offers articles like "The Feel Good Guide: Your Self-Development Calendar," and "How to Turn Your Bored Kids into Happy Little Money Makers."

Even a religious article bears the narcissistic title, "Spiritual Hunger: How to Feed Your Inner Self."

In the *Los Angeles Times* I discover more of the same. A lead article describes the "Samadhi tank," a new kind of "bliss machine." The story says some Californians now climb into these coffin-sized tanks, filled with ten inches of warm water and eight hundred pounds of epsom salts, to float in isolation from light, sound, a sense of time or gravity. After an hour in the tank, one user said, "I went to a party that night and I was so within myself everyone else was an intruder." Designed to produce an eastern mystical experience, the Samadhi tank illustrates American ingenuity applied to the pursuit of pleasures in the inner self.

Looking Out for Number One

A few truths lie scattered through these articles, books, and experiences. But the underlying philosophy apparently is that we exist only for ourselves and must outmaneuver our families, friends, and associates who stand ready to squelch our enjoyment of the good life. About classical Christian virtues like turning the other cheek, suffering for just causes, denying yourself, or caring for others, the writers say little, or they speak of them in ridicule.

For example, Robert J. Ringer, in *Looking Out for No. 1,* tells his readers to make "the conscious, rational effort to spend as much time as possible doing those things which bring you the greatest amount of pleasure and less time on those which cause pain." Ringer has sharp words for family or friends who, through belief in absolute moral standards, might block your quest for pleasure: "No other living person has the right to decide what is moral (right or wrong) for you. I further suggest that you eliminate from your life all individuals who claim—by word or actions, directly or by inference—to possess such a right."

According to this, we evidently discard husbands, wives, parents, or friends—like no-deposit bottles—when they criticize us. Furthermore, since we can't decide right or wrong for anyone else, under Ringer's system we can't condemn Adolf Hitler for slaughtering 6 million Jews. After all, he thought he was right. Ringer tries to escape this dilemma by cautioning that we should never pursue our own pleasure at the expense of other's rights, as Hitler did. But you can't have your cake and eat it, too. If you can't judge others' morality, then you can't tell them to respect people when they don't want to.

How Did We Get This Way?

People have been self-centered and pleasure seeking since the Fall of Man. But rarely have they justified and promoted narcissism so unashamedly as we do today. What has produced this in America? Among many causes, I would like to discuss two: secularism and affluence.

Secularism teaches that God is nonexistent or irrelevant, that nothing has a supernatural cause, and that religion and morality are relative and man-made. Though America has never been an entirely Christian nation, and some of our founding fathers even rejected or attacked traditional Christianity, many biblical teachings have permeated our culture and received at least lip service from the population. Americans have traditionally respected biblical commandments, even if they haven't obeyed them. But, in the twentieth century, European philosophical currents have undercut Christianity and replaced the biblical outlook with secularism. Christianity once influenced American life at its core, but Christ's teachings are now banished to the fringes. Public education, the media, the courts, the government, and even many churches presently dispense the secular view.

As biblical influence has diminished, society has cast off its restraints and today not only practices selfish and immoral behavior, but even encourages and justifies such transgressions. People once respected biblical standards of right and wrong. Now they are unsure there even *is* a right or wrong. By substituting himself for God and his own opinion for biblical commands, modern man has lost his moral moorings. As an athletic contest without rules or referees would degenerate into violence and chaos, so, under the sway of secularism, modern life is sinking deeper into selfishness, anarchy, and brutality.

The county in which I presently live experiences about six youth-gang killings a week. A large portion of my city's public-school teachers now receive "combat pay" as inducement to face the dangers of their once-safe classrooms. Multiple murders in our area of the state now make the Charles Manson killings look tame. Over the last three years alone, we have been terrorized by the "trash-bag murder," who stuffed victims' remains into trash bags; the "hillside strangler," who scattered mutilated bodies over hillside areas; and the "skid-row slasher," who slit the throats of skid-row derelicts. Between them, these three killers probably murdered more than fifty persons. Presently police are searching for a new one, "the Orange Coast rapist," who rapes and then bludgeons to death young women in first-floor apartments. Though secularism may not directly advocate such violence, its amoral philosophy removes the restraints that check this dark side of human nature.

A Parallel Case

A biblical parallel to the effects of secularism comes from the Book of Judges. Filled with murder, rape, violence, and even human dismemberment, this grisly document describes Israel's apostasy more than a thousand years before Christ. The last words of Judges, ". . . everyone did what was right *in his own eyes" (italics mine)*, summarize Robert Ringer's philosophy and state why life became so savage in that distant era. As each Israelite devoted himself solely to Number One, family unity dissolved, community stability collapsed, and government effectiveness evaporated. Foreign tyrannies again reduced the once-proud Israelites to slavery. If America pursues the philosophy of looking out for Number One to its logical end, a similar fate awaits us.

In contrast, a small appendix to Judges, the Book of Ruth, describes a young Moabite woman who lived for something beyond her own ego. Ruth's immortal words to her Jewish mother-in-law, Naomi, are often repeated as wedding vows and beautifully portray devotion to another's welfare: ". . . where you go, I will go, and where you lodge, I will lodge. Your people shall be my people, and your God, my God. Where you die, I will die, and there I will be buried. Thus may the Lord do to me, and worse, if anything but death parts you and me" (Ruth 1:16, 17). How many of us today would so lay down our lives for someone else, and our mothers-in-law at that!

The Curse of Wealth

A second cause of our national narcissism is the affluence spawned by modern technology. Technology allows today's average person to enjoy laborsaving devices, leisure time, mobility, and freedom from pain that a king of two centuries ago would have envied. But, along with these benefits, technology has engulfed us in wealth and helped create a materialistic, pleasure-oriented, consumer society. To sell the goods produced by American factories, Madison Avenue beckons us toward a self-centered, pleasure-oriented "good life," where instant gratification reigns, and pain, duty, and sacrifice barely exist. Such materialistic hedonism combines with godless secularism to become a deadly poison in the nation's bloodstream. This mixture helps create a self-centered society so addicted to its own pleasure that it cannot survive long.

A Different Approach

The New Testament calls us to an approach radically different from the secular, materialistic, looking out for Number One philosophy. Two of Jesus' disciples once requested ". . . Grant that we may sit in Your glory, one on Your right, and one on Your left" (Mark 10:37). They were following Jesus with a me-first mentality. Jesus used the incident to instruct them and their fellow disciples about selfless service: ". . . You know that those who are recognized as rulers of the Gentiles lord it over them; and their great men exercise authority over them. But it is not so among you, but whoever wishes to become great among you shall be your servant; and whoever wishes to be first among you shall be slave of all. For even the Son of Man did not come to be served, but to serve, and to give His life a ransom for many" (Mark 10:42–45).

Jesus pointed out that people climb all over each other to gain position and then exercise their authority with a vengeance. When Jesus spoke of how the gentiles "lord" their positions, Mark used the Greek work *katakurieuo,* which means "superlord." In government, in business, in the church, even in the home, many "superlord" it over one another as they look out for Number One and try to make everything go their way. Jesus said that true greatness comes from serving, even being another's slave. Then He illustrated it from His own life: He did not come into the world for a pampered, smooth, pain-free existence, but to serve, to suffer, even to die.

The night before His crucifixion, He again instructed the disciples in humility. He disrobed Himself, took a towel, and washed their feet. Ancient protocol dictated that servants should wash the feet of guests, when they came in off the dirty, unpaved streets. No servant was present, so Jesus assumed the servant's role. According to custom, with no servant present, the disciples should wait on their teacher. But Jesus reversed the roles, to wait on the disciples. Then He told the disciples, "You call Me Teacher and Lord; and you are right; for so I am. If I then, the Lord and the Teacher, washed your feet, you also ought to wash one another's feet. For I gave you an example that you also should do as I did to you" (John 13:13–15).

Social stratification, disparity between rich and poor, even worship of kings and emperors permeated ancient society. Jesus instructed His followers to perform humble service in such a haughty, power-hungry world. Then He set the ultimate example by serving, and even dying for, that world.

Refusing to Be Number One

Jesus' humility deeply affected the once-arrogant apostle Paul. To some bickering church members in Philippi, he wrote:

> Have this attitude in yourselves which was also in Christ Jesus, who, although He existed in the form of God, did not regard equality with God a thing to be grasped, but emptied Himself, taking the form of a bondservant. . . . He humbled Himself by becoming obedient to the point of death, even death on a cross.
> Philippians 2:5–8

When Paul said Jesus did not consider equality with God something ". . . to be grasped . . .," he used a word which usually means "to seize by force." For example, the verb from which it comes describes the crowd's impulsive attempt to crown Jesus a king in John 6:15: ". . . they were intending to come and *take Him by force,* to make Him king . . ." *(italics mine).* Paul seems to say that Jesus did not wish to seize equality with God the Father, by force. Though Jesus is equal in His being to the Father, as second person of the Trinity, He takes a subordinate position.

We can illustrate equality of being but subordination of position within contemporary politics. We regularly elect a president of the United States, whom no one assumes is a being superior to the rest of us. In fact, we may feel we could have done better, in many areas, than some of our presidents! But we do assume a subordinate position to the president, and most of us will submit to his authority, as he constitutionally exercises it.

Jesus is equal in being to God the Father, yet eternally subordinate in position. In eternity future "... the Son Himself also will be subjected to the One [that is, God the Father] who subjected all things to Him, that God may be all in all" (1 Corinthians 15:28). Jesus refused to seize first place in the Trinity, stooped to become a man, and then rose to become king of the universe, under the Father's authority. Jesus humbled Himself and ascended to the heights. In contrast, Adam grabbed the fruit, tried to promote himself to God's level, and then sank to the depths.

The Servant Role

Jesus' humility is our example. Instead of looking out for Number One, we must serve. A young minister once told me that, during his first few years out of seminary, he mistakenly wanted to make a name for himself. Unfortunately, many pastors, churches, and Christian organizations also want to make names for themselves. Jesus said "... every one who exalts himself shall be humbled ..." (Luke 18:14).

Husbands and Wives

A me-first philosophy subtly works its way into our marriages, as well as our churches. Many people marry, not to serve their partners, but so that their partners can serve them. Many a man secretly wants a wife who will instantly gratify his sexual needs, patiently put up with his foibles, lovingly massage his ego, and cheerfully lift family responsibilities off his back. Many a woman secretly longs for a husband who will graciously submit to her suggestions, constantly envelop her with love, generously supply her with money, and confidently lead her in the Christian life. When each partner realizes that his or her mate falls painfully short of such expectations, disillusionment, anger, and—frequently—divorce follow. Instead of breaking up, such couples should scale down their unrealistic hopes and cease demanding that their partners satisfy all their needs. Each should start to give, instead of just expecting to get.

A housewife complained to one of my friends that she wanted to leave her husband because he didn't make her happy. My friend wisely replied that God wants us to be righteous more than He wants us to be happy. Jesus said, "Blessed are those who hunger and thirst for *righteousness . . .*" (Matthew 5:6, *italics mine*), not, "Blessed are those who hunger and thirst for *happiness.*"

God's purpose, for some Christians, may even include unhappy marriages, where their lifetime dreams never come true. This grates against the romantic, idealistic notions we've cherished from childhood. We don't plan on unhappy marriages, but other Christians must endure being bereaved, unmarried, sick, or senile, and they didn't plan on these things, either. Jesus endured the cross. We live in a fallen world, not a rose garden.

I certainly sympathize with those who have selfish, immature, thoughtless mates, though I feel I enjoy a happy marriage. I realize some people come home to disappointment and heartache whenever they open their front doors. Yet some of the greatest Christians have endured painful family problems and still had fulfilled lives. John Wesley's insanely jealous wife repeatedly and unjustly accused him of adultery. She would steal letters he wrote to women sincerely seeking spiritual counsel, add her own comments, then mail them to his enemies for publication. A shocked co-worker of Wesley's once came upon Mrs. Wesley, running after her husband, yanking out his hair by the roots. Fortunately for Wesley, she finally deserted him. The wife of William Carey, the father of modern missions, became mentally unbalanced and kept their marriage in turmoil during his first years in India, when he most needed her encouragement and support. The husband of Hannah Whitall Smith, author of the spiritual classic, *The Christian's Secret of a Happy Life,* spent the last twenty-five years of their marriage disillusioned and bitter with God, though he had once been a famous Christian speaker. Perhaps this contributed to their daughter's unwise marriage to Bertrand Russell, the famous atheist.

Though important, marriage is not all there is to life. Many couples demand too much happiness from matrimony. In a fallen world, two fallen people, even at their best, cannot satisfy all each other's needs.

Parents and Children

Parents and children should also learn to serve each other. God gives parents authority over children, so they do not serve their children by relinquishing authority, but by properly exercising it. Paul says we should raise our children ". . . in the discipline and instruction of the Lord" (Ephesians 6:4). This requires sacrifice, work, and firmness.

I know of one family whose children run wild. The parents, occupied with their own affluent life-style of traveling, attending parties, and going skiing, often do not know where their children are, what they are doing, or whom they are with. Liberally supplied with money and permissive baby-sitters, the children raise themselves. Proverbs 29:15 (NIV) warns, "The rod of correction imparts wisdom, but a child left to itself disgraces his mother." Such parents neglect, not serve, their children. Because they supply the children with shelter, clothing, and finances, they fool themselves into thinking they are expressing love. Today, millions of physically healthy American children suffer emotional neglect from parents too busy to serve them by being involved in their lives.

Other parents are harsh and overcontrolling. Several years ago one of my daughters had a birthday party in our backyard, to which she invited her neighborhood friends. In the middle of the party, one child's mother rushed in and scolded and spanked her daughter in front of all the others. Such public humiliation deeply wounded the little girl's spirit. Paul tells parents not to exasperate their children (Ephesians 6:4). Overcontrol, unreasonable regulations, and explosive anger exact a heavy toll from the sensitive spirit of a child. Scripture advises a proper mix of tenderness with discipline, and firmness with flexibility, in child raising. We usually mix too much of one, with too little of the other.

Children should also learn to serve their parents, especially as the children grow older and are more able to help. All our parents made mistakes in raising us. We make mistakes in raising our own children. Some grown children still resent the parent who failed them in early life. Perhaps the parent deserted the family to marry someone else, drank too much, or disciplined too harshly. We must be like God: forgive and forget.

I know a woman in her thirties who has spent most of her life rebelling against an overcontrolling father. Whatever he likes, she likes the opposite. He is a conservative Republican; she is a liberal Democrat. He wanted her to marry a businessman; she chose an artist. He doesn't like foreigners; she married a man from the Middle East. She is trying to prove she's free of her father, but he still determines many of her decisions, for she feels bound to choose the opposite of what he likes.

Rebellious children are not free children, since they are rarely free to agree with their parents. "Honor your father and mother" is still valid. If we serve like Jesus, we will serve and honor our parents, whether they deserve it or not.

Unnecessary Submission

Though we should reject the me-first philosophy and serve one another, we sometimes face situations in which serving and submitting become unnecessary or even destructive. Paul wrote to Corinthian slaves, "Were you called while a slave? Do not worry about it; but if you are able also to become free, rather do that" (1 Corinthians 7:21). He told some of the Corinthians to submit to slavery without complaint. When a life condition is unalterable, we should quietly accept it as God's will. Some people are lifelong invalids. Christians in Marxist societies frequently cannot advance economically or educationally. In such cases, we can look to Jesus, who suffered more unjustly than we ever will, yet, ". . . while being reviled, He did not revile in return; while suffering, He uttered no threats, but kept entrusting Himself to Him who judges righteously" (1 Peter 2:23).

But when we can alter unfavorable conditions, we should not hesitate, for Paul also encouraged the Corinthian slaves actively to seek freedom, when possible. God may call us to suffer unjustly, but he does not call us to suffer unnecessarily. I remember talking with a student who worked part-time at an ice-cream store, to pay school expenses. The manager paid meager wages and pressured her to work after hours, without giving her extra pay. Being compliant and loyal, she hesitated to quit and find a better job. I encouraged her to seek other work: God wants us to improve our status, when we can do so legitimately.

Destructive Submission

On other occasions, submission is even destructive. Sometimes we must refuse to submit to the state. Jewish leaders commanded early Christians to stop spreading the Gospel (Acts 4:13–22). Fortunately, the early Christians refused to comply. We never obey the state, if it means disobeying God.

Sometimes we encounter false teaching. Neither Paul nor Jesus advocated quietly submitting to heresy. Instead the Bible tells us to resist and protest, as Jesus did against the Pharisees.

Occasionally we cannot even submit and serve in a marriage. One young woman I know was savagely tortured, as a little girl, by her alcoholic father, when she was only four. He would heat a screwdriver on the stove, then place her hand on it. Unfortunately, a pastor encouraged the mother not to separate the girl from her father. The girl suffered deep emotional scars because of such foolish advice.

Incest is a growing problem today. When I encounter it in counseling, I urge immediate separation of the child from the offending parent, to protect that child from the sexual and emotional confusion incest causes.

I do not approve of family breakups just because people cannot get along, make each other happy, and fulfill each other's dreams. Easy divorce and rebellious children are rotting the foundations of American family life. But, in a fallen world, physical brutality, incest, or similar disastrous circumstances may force families apart. (Sometimes the Law of Moses ordered sexual offenders or physical abusers executed.) God calls us to submit, but, when human life and welfare are at stake, sometimes we must seek drastic solutions.

God calls us to intelligent serving and submitting, instead of looking out for Number One and exalting ourselves. Pride and selfishness, at first glance, may seem the way to go. You get what you want. You're the center of attention. But serving, as Christ did, has beauty, dignity, and strength. Ultimately it has more power than arrogance, more satisfaction than self-centeredness, more joy than egotism.

He served us; we should serve one another.

10
THE WAY OF FAITH

On May 25, 1979, American Airlines Flight 191 lifted off from Chicago's O'Hare Airport for Los Angeles. Passengers anticipated a smooth flight and arrival just in time for the Memorial Day weekend. But, shortly after takeoff, the huge DC-10 lost an engine, rolled on its side, and fell to earth like a giant, wounded bird, taking 273 lives down with it. Among the victims were the husband of a teacher at our local grade school and a business executive who attended our church.

Subsequent media reports suggested that faulty design and improper maintenance contributed to the crash. Such grim tragedies remind us that we live by faith in others and continually trust our lives to others' hands. When misfortunes take the lives of loved ones, we realize how misplaced our faith was. But, despite mishaps, we continue to place faith in people, for we cannot function otherwise in life. Our choice is not whether or not to have faith, but in whom or. cwhat to have faith.

Consider the faith we must have to drive to the supermarket, buy groceries, and return home. We must stake our lives on our cars' steering and brakes working properly. We must have faith that oncoming drivers will avoid smashing into us head-on. We must have faith the groceries we purchase will not poison our families, though we don't know who grew, transported, or canned the food, and probably don't know who manages the supermarket. We must have faith our empty and unguarded houses are safe to return to, though a thief, murderer, or rapist could be waiting there.

Naive Faith

Faith is an essential ingredient of life. Yet we try to avoid believing in what is untrustworthy, untrue, or unsubstantiated. Sally, a plain-looking, shy young woman, sought my wife's counsel and unloaded on her a bizarre story of how she had suffered parental abuse, engaged in wild orgies, gotten pregnant, and now wanted an abortion. By chance, my wife discovered Sally had grown up in an average home, dated rarely, and lived an uneventful, rather dull life. Sally became a compulsive liar because she relished the attention she attracted through her wild tales; plus she probably longed, unconsciously, to engage in some of the rebellious behavior she described. Until Sally repented of her lying and proved herself truthful, over time, it would be foolish to believe her. We cannot naively trust anyone and everyone, for the world is filled with fallen, devious people.

The secularist, however, usually assumes that the Christian is naive, blindly trusting in primitive myths and fairy tales, while closing his eyes to scientific evidence, because he probably needs a crutch with which to face life. Yet the secularist lives by faith as much as the Christian. Not only does he live by faith in everyday life, but he builds his secular philosophy with bricks of faith, for he cannot prove there is no God, no eternal soul, no absolute morality, no heaven or hell. The issue is not who lives by faith, but whose faith has the most reasonable and sensible foundation.

Believing in Our Creator

When we compare the Christian's foundation with that of the secularist, I am convinced the secularist is the naive believer in mythical and unsubstantiated assertions. For example, the Christian believes the universe, nature, and humanity did not just happen; God created them. If I notice some leaves randomly scattered over my lawn, one here, another there, I assume their scattering happened by chance, as the wind blew. But if I see a wristwatch accidentally dropped on my lawn, I assume that someone designed and manufactured the watch. Unlike the random pattern of the leaves, the watch has gears, springs, numbers, hands, and finely engineered parts precisely fitted together for its accurate and smooth operation. Such a watch could never happen, not if I waited 10 billion years. Someone had to design and make it.

Yet the simplest living cell is infinitely more complex and organized than that watch. Then consider that the human eye outperforms our best cameras; the human heart, our most well-designed motors; and the human brain, our most sophisticated computers. How could the cell, the eye, the heart, the brain, just evolve by chance? They could no more happen than the watch. To believe they happened by chance is *really* to have a naive, unsophisticated faith.

Dr. Francis Crick, eminent Nobel Prize winner, who helped crack the DNA code, recently tried to resolve the impossibility of life starting by chance by proposing that some outer-space civilization traveled to earth and planted life here. But this raises more questions than it answers. Who created life in that civilization? Do we have solid evidence that outer-space beings came here, planted life, and left? The Nobel Prize winner's view demands far more blind faith than the viewpoint of Genesis does!

Believing in Jesus and the Bible

Christians also believe Jesus Christ was no mere man, but God's Son. The four Gospels state that Jesus repeatedly claimed to be God's Son. Does His claim scientifically prove

He is God incarnate? No, but consider the alternatives. If He were not God's Son, then He was either lying or deluded in such a claim. But why should Jesus deceive us, when He had nothing to gain by it? His claim got Him crucified. Then, when we study Jesus' life and teachings, we soon realize He was the greatest, wisest, best person who ever lived. Can we believe such a person was really an imposter? Can we believe the greatest figure of all time was but a deluded fanatic?

Of course, others say that He never claimed these things—the early church just made up the Jesus we read about. In fact, they say, maybe Jesus never existed. Have you thought of the difficulty of making up a figure like Jesus? Who today or back then could think up the Sermon on the Mount, the parable of the good Samaritan, or the story of the prodigal son? He who gave such teachings was a spiritual genius. Only someone as great as Jesus could make Jesus up! To have faith in Jesus as the Son of God is not blind; it makes sense.

Christians also believe the Bible is God's Word and the authority to which they should submit their lives. Again, we cannot scientifically prove this. But Jesus believed the Bible was God's Word; and, if He is God's Son, He must be correct. Furthermore, though written by many different human authors, over many centuries, the Bible's unity, accuracy, profundity, morality, beauty, timelessness, and prophecies show that more than human hands penned its pages. The Christian agrees with Peter that the biblical writers ". . . spoke from God as they were carried along by the Holy Spirit" (2 Peter 1:21 NIV). Our faith in the Bible as God's Word is reasonable, not blind and baseless.

Applying Christianity to Life

Though Christians believe in God, Jesus Christ, and the Bible, most of them have problems applying their faith to

their lives. Instead of clinging steadfastly to biblical promises, they cave in before negative circumstances, destructive
emotions, or secular and relativistic brainwashing.

Some years ago I knew a gifted, brilliant pastor, who had
spent several years studying in the best seminaries. To my
knowledge, he had a loving, supportive family. Unfortunately, he could never resolve some deep emotional problems, became a closet alcoholic, and finally a tragic suicide.
When his body was discovered, next to it was a Bible opened
to 1 Corinthians 9:27 (KJV), "But I keep under my body, and
bring it into subjection: lest that by any means, when I have
preached to others, I myself should be a castaway." This
pastor understood Christianity intellectually, but could not
make it work in his life.

In contrast, the heroes of Scripture, sometimes after much
doubting, stubbornly believed God, though the cards frequently were stacked against them. Abraham, one of the
Bible's greatest examples of faith, was promised a son, though
he and his wife were old and childless. Romans 4:19–21 says:

> . . . without becoming weak in faith he contemplated
> his own body, now as good as dead since he was about a
> hundred years old, and the deadness of Sarah's womb;
> yet, with respect to the promise of God, he did not
> waver in unbelief, but grew strong in faith, giving glory
> to God, and being fully assured that what He had
> promised, He was able also to perform.

Abraham confronted a contradiction: His circumstances
said he could never have a son, yet God's promise said he
would. The Bible says Abraham ". . . contemplated his own
body. . . ." (The King James Version mistranslates it,
". . . he considered not his own body . . .") The word for
"contemplate," *katanoeo* in the Greek, means to "consider
carefully with reflection." Abraham considered carefully

with reflection his wife's age and barrenness. He was a realist; he looked his circumstances straight in the eye. But he looked also at God's promise and decided the divine pledge had power over human circumstances. God rewarded his faith with the child Isaac.

Noah and the Ark

Noah faced a similar plight. God told him he should build an ark, because a flood would sweep the earth. Imagine building a huge ship, visible for blocks, right in your own backyard, while promising skeptical fellow citizens the boat would rescue them from a worldwide flood! So ridiculous did God's promise to Noah seem that not one person climbed on board the ark, except for Noah and his family. Though the laughingstock of his society, Noah favored God's promise over human ridicule, and in the end his jeering neighbors, not Noah, had played the fool. Like Abraham, Noah believed God's promise over negative circumstances and received his reward.

Yet God has probably never personally appeared nor audibly spoken to any of us, promising that this or that would happen, as He did with Abraham and Noah. Though some Christians claim to have had visions in which they heard God speaking, such ecstatic experiences, if valid, are the exception, not the rule. Other Christians may never have heard God's audible voice, but they do seem able to believe God for greater things than the rest of us. Yet again they are the exception and probably possess a special gift of faith. Most of us struggle with our doubts; we feel frustrated because so many prayers apparently go unanswered; and we would give almost anything if, just once, God would personally appear and promise to resolve some of our problems.

Yet even if we never have ecstatic visions or possess special gifts of faith, we can experience revolutionary change in our Christian lives, through believing the general promises of

God in Scripture. What is the difference whether God dramatically makes a promise in a vision or whether He quietly makes it in a Scripture verse? If God makes a promise, He will honor it, no matter when, where, or how He made it. God refused to speak to Elijah through sensational winds, earthquakes, and fires; instead He communicated through a "... gentle whisper" (1 Kings 19:12 NIV).

God Loves Us

One of the most important promises God makes in the Bible is simply that He loves us (*see* 1 John 4:10). Love desires what is best for others, so God always desires what is best for us. This is why He sometimes does not give us what we want: He knows what we want is not best for us. A small boy sees the shiny knife blade and wants to grab it. His mother won't give it to him, because she loves him and knows it will hurt him.

On the other hand, sometimes that which really is best for us is something we don't want. When our children were small, we took them to the doctor often, because they frequently got ear infections. Our children could not understand why the doctor gave them painful shots in their little rear ends, to get rid of pains in their ears. They already had pain in one part of their bodies; how could inflicting pain in another part help? Yet we wanted the doctor to give them shots, because we loved them. My father grew up before the age of antibiotics and suffered permanent hearing loss, because he could not get such shots. God's love, like a wise parent's love, does what is best in the long run, even if it hurts in the short run.

Knowing by Faith

But as we endure the trials of living, we know God loves us—not by how much pleasure or pain circumstances bring, but by God's promises in Scripture. Recently I have been counseling a teenager who has known many heartbreaks. Her father deserted her mother at the girl's birth. At three, her mother allowed relatives to adopt her. At twelve, the relatives got a divorce, and she returned to her natural mother. At fifteen, her natural mother died. Her father's desertion, her relatives' divorce, and her mother's death have left deep scars. She feels deserted and unloved, even by God.

I have tried to help her see that those tragic events are evidences of a fallen world, rather than evidences that God rejects her. Since the world is fallen, life will rarely be fair. Those who apparently deserve punishment in this life often seem to have too easy a time of it. Those who are apparently innocent, especially little children, may meet one misfortune after another. But if only those who "deserve it" suffered tragedy and only those who were "innocent" had life easy, the world would be fair and just, rather than cursed and fallen. Injustice, unfairness, and evil that randomly strike one but not another are part of the fabric of existence in a sinful world. This is why we long for heaven, where justice, fairness, and goodness are at the core of existence.

Life's tragedies do not mean that God hates us; they prove the world is evil. God loves us in the midst of trials and tragedies. "Who shall separate us from the love of Christ? Shall tribulation, or distress, or persecution, or famine, or nakedness, or peril, or sword? . . . But *in* all these things we overwhelmingly conquer through Him who loved us" (Romans 8:35, 37, *italics mine*).

Yet we cannot view life this way, unless we view it through eyes of faith. Like Abraham and Noah, we must believe what *God* says of our circumstances, instead of what *we* think of the circumstances. Abraham contemplated his circumstances, but also contemplated God's word about them. We must do the same.

A Flat Earth?

Recently I read about a press interview with Charles K. Johnson, president of the International Flat Earth Research Society. His society has fifteen hundred members, who pay seven dollars annual dues and receive the society's publication, *The Flat Earth News.* Johnson claims that the earth is flat, the space program is a hoax, and pictures taken from satellites are faked. He says that his wife used to live in Australia, and, if the earth were a globe, she would have fallen off!

Laughable as this sounds, millions down through history have agreed with Charles Johnson. In past times, those who thought the earth was round were considered the crackpots! Didn't it make sense that people would fall off the bottom side, if the earth were a globe? Didn't the land *look* flat?

But now that we can see through the eyes of modern science, we know the earth is round. When we can look at life through the eyes of faith, when we can see ourselves and our circumstances as God sees us, what looks flat also becomes round, so to speak; and, though it appears God does not love us, by faith we understand He does.

The Paranoid Person

Often Christians who have special difficulty believing God loves them are people with paranoid tendencies. Psychotic paranoids or paranoid schizophrenics may end up in institutions (these two psychoses bear some resemblances, but are not the same). But millions are not psychotic, yet have the tendencies of these mental disorders and encounter resulting problems in human relationships.

Those with paranoid tendencies have low self-images and carry heavy loads of unconscious guilt. They are overly sensitive to blame and criticism, take innocent remarks personally, and feel others are against them. They resemble a person carrying several hundred pounds on his back. Adding just a few more pounds to his immense load is often more than he can stand. But, if he carried no load at all, he could easily bear the extra weight. The paranoid personality carries so much self-condemnation that even slight criticism from others adds unbearably to its already oppressive burden.

Paranoid people become their own worst enemies. Believing others dislike them, they behave so hostilely that they end up causing the very dislike they suspect. They try to prove themselves right and worthy by proving everyone else wrong and unworthy.

The Example of Saul

Saul, Israel's first king, had paranoid tendencies. On one occasion Samuel the prophet commanded Saul to exterminate the Amalakites and their possessions. The idolatrous Amalakites had long opposed God and His people, so their judgment was deserved. But the disobedient Saul spared the Amalakite king and kept the best of their farm animals. When Samuel rebuked Saul for his disobedience, Saul defended himself: ". . . I did obey the voice of the Lord. . . . But the people took some of the spoil, sheep and oxen . . . to sacrifice to the Lord . . ." (1 Samuel 15:20, 21). When Samuel further admonished Saul, Saul conceded, ". . . I have sinned . . . because I feared the people and listened to their voice" (v. 24). Saul could not honestly admit that he had goofed. According to Saul, "the people," not he, were really at fault. Later Saul met David, but became insanely suspicious of him, though David repeatedly proved his loyalty. Eventually Saul tried to murder David. Finally Saul lost his kingdom and met a tragic end.

Saul refused to admit his faults. Others, either the people, David, or his own family, were always to blame. Because he thought others were to blame, Saul suspected and attacked them, converting his once-loyal friends into enemies and creating his own downfall. In contrast, when David became king, he probably blundered as often as Saul; but, believing God loved him and having an adequate sense of self-worth, he admitted and repented of his mistakes. None of Israel's kings was more tragic than the suspicious and paranoid Saul, and none was more loved than the benevolent and generous David.

Lack of Faith

At the heart of Saul's problem was his lack of faith. He refused to believe that God really loved and forgave him. Like other paranoids, he had to be right and everyone else wrong. The paranoid person, like Israel of old, seeks to establish his own righteousness, instead of submitting to God's (Romans 10:3).

I know of a Canadian minister with great charisma. Yet relatively few people have heard of him. Like Saul, he cannot grasp that God really loves him. Instead of submitting himself to God, he has tried to carve out his own kingdom, through starting a small, semicultic organization. The organization bears the paranoid marks of its founder; it is hostile toward other Christians and stirs up their hostility toward it. It refuses to admit its own weaknesses, but self-righteously denounces other groups. Like many cults, it reflects the paranoid personality on a group level.

The solution to the paranoid problem is believing God over feelings and circumstances, as Abraham did. Instead of allowing guilt feelings to pile up until he must battle the world, the paranoid needs to accept that God loves and receives him, whether or not he is right. He is adequate in Christ, so he does not have to show himself right by making all others wrong. The message "God really loves me" needs to penetrate the paranoid's tortured soul. Unfortunately, the paranoid usually claims to believe God loves him, but denies it underneath. But, through prayer and therapy, he can begin to open up his closed and closely guarded heart and become a more harmonious member of the human family.

The Way of Freedom

The way of faith is the way of freedom. By believing what God says about us, even though His words seem to contradict our senses, we begin to find who we are, who God is, and how He wants us to live. We feel frustrated, but believe that God, through our riches in Christ, will perfect us in His time. We feel guilty, but believe that God, through Christ, has forgiven us. We feel unacceptable, but believe that God, through grace, welcomes us. We feel inadequate, but believe that God, through union with Christ, makes us OK. We feel worthless, but believe that God, through regeneration, can make us worthwhile. We feel bound, but believe that God has called us to be free.

We don't always find freedom suddenly or without struggle. We cannot find it now perfectly and totally. But Jesus said the truth will set us free, and we can find it.

God will never let us rest until we do.